SAUSSURE

FOR BEGINNERS™

D1015305

BY W. TERRENCE GORDON
ILLUSTRATED BY ABBE LUBELL

Writers and Readers Publishing, Inc.
P.O. Box 461, Village Station
New York, NY 10014

Writers and Readers Limited
9 Cynthia Street
London N1 9JF
England

A Writers and Readers Documentary Comic Book Copyright © 1996

ISBN # 0-86316-195-2

0 1 2 3 4 5 6 7 8 9

Manufactured in the United States of America

SAUSSURE
FOR BEGINNERS™

Contents

The author extends
special thanks to
Walter Hirtle
and
Mike McMahon.

*W*hen Saussure died on 22 February 1913, the students who had attended his lectures at the University of Geneva sensed that the world had lost a genius.

But there was a slight problem:

The genius had not put his lectures into book form to show the world what a genius he was.

So Saussure's students, in one of the most astonishing moves in the history of ideas, took matters into their own hands and decided to write the book <u>for</u> him. By 1916--a little more than three years after Saussure's death, working from the notes they had taken during Saussure's lectures, the students had compiled and published **Cours de linguistique générale** <u>(Course in General Linguistics)</u> under Saussure's name.

Between 1928 and 1983, the book was translated into seventeen languages.

That book "by" Saussure is considered so important that it has made its influence felt in fields as diverse as anthropology, psychoanalysis, literary criticism, and semiotics.

So, clearly, I am a person we should know something about.

*F*erdinand de Saussure was born in Geneva, Switzerland, on 26 November 1857. Of French origins, the Saussure family had moved to Geneva in the 17th century to escape France's persecution of Protestants. Beginning with Nicolas de Saussure (1709-1791), generations of the family distinguished themselves as scholars.

Ferdinand's grandfather, Nicolas-Theodore (1767-1845), a physicist, chemist, naturalist, and professor of geology and mineralogy at the University of Geneva, discovered a mineral and gave it the family name:

SAUSSURITE!

Young Ferdinand--"our" Saussure--was tutored from an early age by Adolphe Pictet (1799-1875), a distinguished linguist in his own right. By age 13, Ferdinand knew French, German, English, and Latin. At age 15, he was already trying his hand at explaining the general system of language.

At the University of Geneva in 1875-76, he studied Latin, Greek, chemistry, theology, and law. (His <u>Course in General Linguistics</u>--we'll just call it the <u>CGL</u> from now on--describes language with comparisons taken not only from chemistry but also from physics, chess, music, natural species, algebra, etc.)

At age 21, Saussure produced the bombshell that first showed his genius. This was (take a deep breath now): *Mémoire sur le système primitif des voyelles dans les langues indo-européennes.*

It's a work showing that proto-Indo-European languages (the ancestor of a vast family of languages of Europe, India, and southwest Asia) **did not have just three vowels, but five.** What makes this amazing is that young Ferdinand saw the mistake that so many scholars had just kept on repeating and corrected it on a theoretical hunch. It wasn't till years later that very sophisticated equipment used for studying the sounds of language showed that he was absolutely correct.

After being awarded a doctorate at the University of Leipzig, Germany, in 1880, Saussure began his teaching career in Paris, where he stayed until he was called home to be a professor at the University of Geneva in 1891. There he would give a course in the ancient Sanskrit language for 21 years. It could have been a quiet and comfortable career, but the university authorities shook Saussure up by asking him to teach a course on general linguistics.

The very idea frightened him, but he could hardly say no, and he gave the course three times between 1907 and 1911.

He had worked out the main lines of it in 1890 and told his students frankly that he had added nothing since then. He was discouraged by the difficulty of the subject matter and did not really want to return to it. He honestly believed he had nothing worth saying about general linguistics.

This bleak self-appraisal did not improve as Saussure taught his course, and he **systematically destroyed his lecture notes**. The opinion of others was higher:

Fellow-linguist Antoine Meillet said that Saussure "saw scientific matters with the clear blue eyes of the poet and the visionary."

Even before World War II, Saussure's work had already deeply influenced European linguists such as **Gustave Guillaume, Roman Jakobson,** and others. That influence spread to the United States with Jakobson's move to Columbia University and then to Harvard.

In the 1950s, Saussure's ideas began to exert an influence beyond linguistics. **Roland Barthes'** early work in semiotics put Saussure's principles into application. **Claude Lévi-Strauss,** who learned of Saussure's work through Jakobson, adapted the principles to anthropology. Psychiatry and literary criticism are also marked by Saussure's thought in the work of **Jacques Lacan** and **Jacques Derrida**.

Jacques Derrida

Though the degree to which these and other scholars have acknowledged Saussure's influence varies greatly, the currents and development of twentieth century thought are illuminated and enriched by a study of his teachings.

Jacques Derrida consults a spirit medium

Do you think you could reach Ferdinand de Saussure for me?

Medium: "What do you want to ask him?"

Clarification of a passage in the Course in General Linguistics.

Medium: "...I'm getting a good connection...Go ahead."

You said that the idea or phonic substance that a sign contains is of less importance than the other signs that surround it, and that the proof of this is that the value of a term may be modified without either its meaning or its sound being affected... .

I said that?

Well, maybe not. Your students compiled the *Course in General Linguistics* from their own lecture notes after you died.*

There's a piece of reading I'd better catch up on. Try me again tomorrow...

* Although the first edition of Saussure's *Course* was published in 1916, three years after his death, the manuscript sources, showing the variations among the students' lecture notes, were not published till 1968. Emile Constantin's notes, taken when Saussure gave his course for the third and last time in 1910-11, were published only in 1994.

Crystal ball goes dark.

Medium : "System warning: end display of signifiers."

Derrida, wide-eyed with excitement:
"Did he say 'endless play of signifiers?'"

Medium: "Don't quote me on that."

Linguistics is analysis of language, and the linguists who do it show up everywhere to get their data. They may want to study any **part** of language, from sounds to sentence patterns. Or they may want to analyze any **use** of language, from the pronunciation exercises that babies invent for themselves to those baffling streams of speech in the religious experience known as "speaking in tongues." Some linguists study one language and how its sounds vary in different places in a sound-group ("P" for example, is not pronounced in exactly the same way at the beginning of a word -- "pot," and at the end -- "top"). Some may examine the street slang of their own neighborhoods), but their colleagues may race to a far corner of the world to record conversations among the last few speakers of a dying language.

This is all modern linguistics, twentieth century linguistics, as it has been practiced since Saussure's time -- and in many respects because of his influence. So far-reaching has this influence been that Saussure is often called the father of modern linguistics. But what about earlier? Is it not possible that people have been **thinking about language** for almost as long as they have been **using it**? Could it not be that as soon as arboreal man interpreted the grunt of his neighbor as meaning "move further down the branch so that I can sit down too," he began to reflect on that act of interpretation? While lessons from the father of modern linguistics will show us why he had no forebearers this far back in time, we do find linguistic terminology and linguistic investigation thriving in the generation preceding Saussure's -- and we find the first flowering of linguistic thought twenty-two centuries before that!

Modern linguists show up in all sorts of different places.

11

The French word "linguistique," as a noun, had already been in use for at least 24 years when Saussure

was born; its English cousin "linguistic" appeared first in 1837 in the writings of the British scholar William Whewell, who defined it as the science of language. Under the influence of American scholars such as Noah Webster and Dwight Whitney, 'linguistic' was transformed into "linguistics."

By comparison with "linguistic," "linguist" has a prac

tically hoary history: It was first used by Shakespeare in 1591 in *Two Gentlemen of Verona* to mean "one who is skilled in the use of language." Fifty years later, John Wilkins gave the term the meaning "student of language." Language scholars were known as 'philologists' before 'linguist' became the term of choice, and the two terms continued in use alongside each other

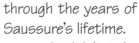

through the years of Saussure's lifetime.

It didn't take

the invention of the terms "linguist" and "linguistics" for the analytic study of language to begin. The link between logic and language in Aristotle's work and the categories he established mark the beginning of what would eventually be

called linguistics. The debate over whether language is **natural** (do we call a table a table because that's the way it is?) or **conventional** (do we call it a table because that's what we decided to call it?) in Plato's *Cratylus* is the very question that opens Saussure's teachings and ties them together.

Before we start looking at the principles Saussure taught, we need to get clear about what he meant by the term "sign."

DEFINITION OF THE LINGUISTIC SIGN

"No Smoking" doesn't cover it. A red slash through a cigarette in a circle doesn't cover it. Pictures, diagrams, graphs, maps, gestures, traffic lights, license plates -- **all** of these are SIGNS.

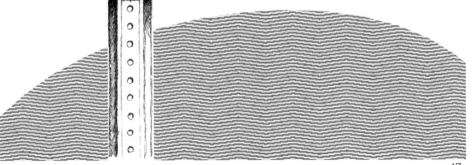

Anything that tells us about something other than itself is a SIGN.

Why "other than itself?" Because the jagged line on a graph isn't there to make you think about jagged lines; it's there to show sales going up and down, or the stock market fluctuating, etc. The red light at an intersection isn't there to make you think about redness; it's there to make you stop. When we speak or write, the sounds we make or the words on the page aren't there just as sounds or ink marks; they bring ideas to our minds.

Words are SIGNS too. When we discuss words, and take them as examples of SIGNS, we should call them "LINGUISTIC SIGNS," but usually it just gets shortened to "SIGNS."

When Saussure sat down to prepare his lecture notes for the course in general linguistics he had been asked to teach, he did not undertake a high and wide survey of linguistic thinking from ancient times. He makes no mention of Plato's *Cratylus*. But one excessively imaginative historian of linguistics does speculate that Saussure was influenced by **Buddhist philosophy**!

Saussure was too dissatisfied with the results produced by earlier linguists to base his teaching on their work. They had failed to ask the question Saussure puts at the beginning and at the end of all his teaching:

What is the nature of the subject matter under study in linguistics?

How could such a basic and important question have been overlooked?

Mainly because linguists had confined their interest to the historical study of language -- its **origins,** its growth, the changes it underwent -- and especially because linguistic analysis had always been based on w r i t t e n   t e x t s. Saussure asked his students to examine instead the spoken word as a starting point for understanding the unique and absolute individuality of e v e r y expressive act. This led to the first of the pairs of terms that Saussure used to develop a framework for linguistics -- the difference between LANGUE (what we can do with language) and PAROLE (what we do with language when we speak).

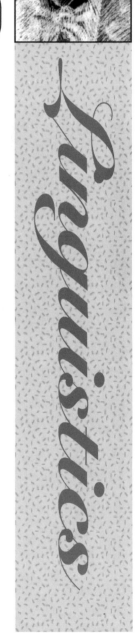

This distinction can be made in English through the terms **LANGUAGE** and **SPEECH**. Many languages distinguish between these and did so before Saussure came on the scene, but linguists had never grounded their analyses here.

This was the great flaw that Saussure saw in even the best of earlier approaches to linguistics, the flaw that he set out to correct. Once **LANGUAGE** versus **SPEECH** was taken as a starting point, it opened the way for Saussure to make further distinctions **within language**. This set a direction for linguistics that was completely different from the one taken by nineteenth century historical linguists. Saussure did not abandon historical linguistics in his teaching, but he did not limit himself to it.

In what other ways did Saussure innovate?

Answer:

By linking linguistics to the more general study of signs (**Reminder**: a SIGN is anything that stands for something other than itself), by identifying features of language as mental entities, by stressing the creativity of language, by establishing a terminology for linguistics that favored carefully defined general terms over technical ones, by a teaching technique that made free use of analogies for features of language drawn from fields as varied as music, chess, mountaineering, and the solar system. In this way, he added imagination to critical scrutiny of his nineteenth century predecessors and

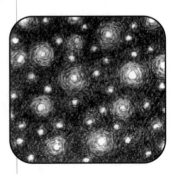

brought linguistics into the twentieth century.

After an introduction beginning with a history of linguistics, tailored to Saussure's criticisms, and ending with **PHONOLOGY** (the sound system of language), the work is divided into five parts. The first of these presents general principles, working through from the nature of the **LINGUISTIC SIGN** to the complementary levels of linguistic analysis. Here Saussure starts by saying that language has too often been taken as nothing other than **NOMENCLATURE** (a list of terms corresponding to things; naming things). He corrects this view as follows:

The **LINGUISTIC SIGN** *does not link a name and a thing, but a* **CONCEPT** *and an* **ACOUSTIC IMAGE.**

Why did Saussure decide that the nomenclature view of language was inadequate?

First of all because it is an over-simplification of the processes of interaction between *mind, world, and words* at the time that language came into being. It assumes that humans already had ideas and that they simply put words to these ideas. This is the linguistic equivalent of imposing the final word on whether the chicken or the egg came first.

Saussure's intuition told him that just as the chicken might have been the egg's idea for getting more eggs, the emergence of ideas and words must have occurred under a process of mutual influence.

So, on the one hand, the nomenclature view takes too little into account. But

it is also vague, giving no indication if the name linked to a thing is basically a psychic entity (Saussure's term for a mental entity shared by the community of speakers who use it to communicate with each other) or a vocal entity (a sound or sequence of sounds). For Saussure, working his way toward the distinction between LANGUAGE and SPEECH, the vagueness of the nomenclature view would not do.

The linguistic SIGN would have to be defined for **LANGUAGE** (the system itself) in a way that would exclude the actual sounds of **SPEECH** (the system put to use).

Saussure's definition, where the LINGUISTIC SIGN has only two components, is no more complex than the nomenclature view that he criticized as being too simple.

In fact, he admits that he found the two-part sign of the nomenclature view appealing. It was only the oversimplification of the processes involved in the birth of language that needed to be avoided.

O.K., I admit it.

TRUMPET

Saussure side-steps this problem in his definition of the SIGN, replacing the fuzzy term NAME from the nomenclature view by ACOUSTIC IMAGE (the mental image of a name that allows a language-user to say the name) and banishing THING in favor of CONCEPT, so that the definition will pair two entities that belong to LANGUAGE. It's a definition that solves the problems Saussure saw with the nomenclature view, but at the expense of eliminating THINGS -- the world that language is used to refer to. It would not be long after the <u>CGL</u> was published that Saussure came in for criticism over his definition.

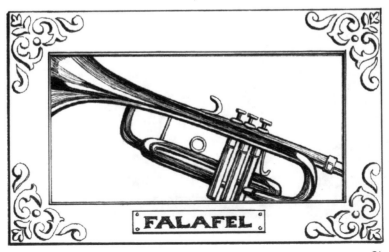

FALAFEL

Once Saussure got the sign defined to his satisfaction as an entity with two parts, he decided to change their names from CONCEPT and ACOUSTIC IMAGE, to SIGNIFIED and SIGNIFIER, respectively. In the original French the terms are **signifié** and **signifiant**, which translate literally as "signified" and "signifying."

Why choose terms that are so similar and run the risk of confusion? Saussure believed that the minimal difference in form between the names of the two parts of the sign would serve to emphasize the contrast between them, as well as the contrast between each of them and the sign as a whole.

SIGNIFIED
(formerly "CONCEPT")

SIGNIFIER
(formerly "ACOUSTIC IMAGE")

Ogden: You say the linguistic sign has <u>two</u> parts?

Saussure: Correct.

Richards: A "<u>concept</u>" linked to an "<u>acoustic image</u>?"

Saussure: Also correct.

Ogden: A "<u>signified</u>" linked to a "<u>signifier</u>?"

Saussure: Correct again!

Richards: And both are "<u>mental entities</u>?"

Saussure: Yes! Yes!

Ogden: But then the process of interpretation is built right into the sign.

Saussure: What do you mean?

Richards: If the signified and the signifier are both mental entities, you've cut your linguistic sign off from any connection with the world outside the mind.

Saussure: You seem to forget that I've defined the sign in a way that will allow the distinction between the language system and speech.

Ogden: But when you go from language to speech, the real world that you have detached from the sign will still be missing.

Saussure: Maybe you two should write your own book.

Richards: As a matter of fact...

Ogden: Ivor, this isn't the place for free publicity.

*The definition of the **SIGN** and the question of what its parts are called are just preliminaries to what Saussure called his first principle:*

 HE LINGUISTIC SIGN IS <u>ARBITRARY</u>

The LINGUISTIC SIGN is **Arbitrary.** Rivers of ink have flowed in the discussion of this notion. To keep clear about what Saussure meant by it, we have to remember that his SIGN has two parts, and that what is arbitrary (determined by choice; randomly chosen) is **making the connection** between them. Language can make any connection it chooses.

When the first language came into existence, when the first word (SIGN) came into existence, any sound or sequence of sounds (SIGNIFIER) could have been chosen to express any concept (SIGNIFIED). The proof of arbitrariness is that when different languages came into existence they developed different SIGNS, different links between SIGNIFIERS and SIGNIFIEDS. If the LINGUISTIC SIGN were not arbitrary, there would be only one language in the world.

But even though the SIGN is arbitrary as far as the connection between its SIGNIFIER and SIGNIFIED goes, it is not arbitrary for language users. If it were, everybody could come up with whatever SIGNS they wanted, and communication would break down.

The principle of the arbitrariness of the linguistic SIGN operates in connection with Saussure's second principle:

(The Signifier is <u>Linear</u>)

"Linear" makes us think of space, and a printed SIGNIFIER (such as any of the words you are reading here) is linear. But Saussure is thinking primarily of *time* when he says 'linear.' A spoken SIGNIFIER is just as linear as a written one, because whenever it is more complex than a single sound (which is almost always the case), it occurs in a sequence over time. That makes it linear. Compare the following examples:

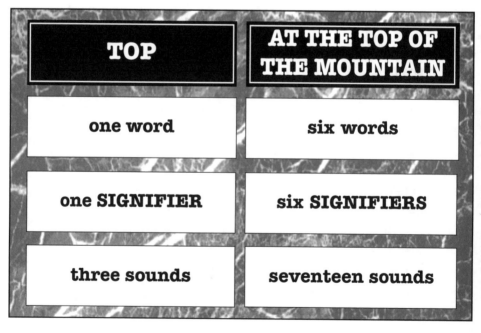

TOP	AT THE TOP OF THE MOUNTAIN
one word	six words
one SIGNIFIER	six SIGNIFIERS
three sounds	seventeen sounds

The second example is more complex, but both are linear.

Saussure does not give many details in discussing the principle of linearity, but he tells us that the operation of language depends on it. He goes so far as to say that its consequences are profound, and in fact they are. Why? Because linearity keeps us from seeing or hearing a SIGNIFIER or SIGNIFIERS all at once. The big difference between the *linearity* of the SIG-NIFIER and the *arbitrariness* of the SIGN is that the first is like a *chain*, but the second is just one link.

HOW AND WHY THE LINGUISTIC SIGN IS *UNCHANGEABLE*

Saussure moves on from his concept of the two-part SIGN to the relationship between the SIGN and its users. Here he detects a *paradox* (a statement that seems contrary to common sense but is nonetheless probably true): language is free to set up a link between any sound (or sequence of sounds) and any idea, but once the link is made, neither an individual speaker nor the whole community of speakers is free to undo it. They are not free to replace that link by another one either.

For example: the English language could have chosen some other sequence of sounds than the three in "top" to express the idea of the highest part of an object (and other languages did), but now it is here to stay. Governments cannot legislate a word out of existence. Why? Because it was never legislated **into** existence.

There are other ways to explain why LINGUISTIC SIGNS cannot be modified at will, but Saussure prefers the one linked to a principle he has already set out -- the arbitrariness of the SIGN. Since the SIGN is arbitrary, there is no reason to prefer one particular SIGNIFIER-SIGNIFIED combination over any other. Arbitrariness makes it impossible to argue the relative merits of SIGNS in any rational way.

How could all the speakers of English be convinced to start using some other way of expressing the idea of "top"?

It will never work, you know. The SIGN is arbitrary.

Yeah! Well, maybe I could get a better sign, brighter paint, bolder typeface...

No, no! I mean the linguistic sign. The word "top" is a sign. Sounds linked to a concept. Its arbitrariness keeps it in place in the language system.

The Establishment's in on this arbitrariness thing, right?

It isn't easy teaching linguistics.

*H*OW AND WHY THE LINGUISTIC SIGN IS *CHANGEABLE*

Over time, language and its SIGNS change. New SIGNIFIER-SIGNIFIED links may replace old ones or add to their number. "Tide" used to mean "period" or "season," now it means "periodic rise and fall of water level"; "mouse" used to mean only a type of small rodent, till personal computers were invented and brought with them a new meaning of "mouse" that coexists comfortably with the old one.

Saussure has just finished teaching us that the SIGNIFIER-SIGNIFIED link is arbitrary and that this arbitrariness **prevents** linguistic change **by design**; now it appears that the same arbitrariness **permits** language to change. If the SIGN were not arbitrary, the new meanings of "tide" and "mouse" could never have developed.

The arbitrariness of the SIGN is a tough concept. Saussure had to start with it because other principles turn out to be a necessary consequence of it.

Linguistics can study language AT ONE POINT IN TIME or ITS DEVELOPMENT OVER TIME.

Saussure talks about two ways of analyzing language -- SYNCHRONIC and DIACHRONIC. Why did he choose these terms? If you know the Latin words they come from, you can answer this question, but nowadays most people don't know Latin. (Latin: Synchronous = same time; Diachronous = through time.)

Over time, language evolves and signs do change.

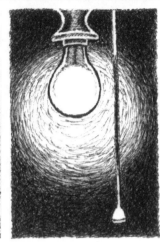

So let's clarify by asking the same question about names for dogs. Why Spot? Obviously, because the dog has spots on his body? Why Rover? Because he likes to rove. Here is a pair of names you can do something with. Since SYNCHRONIC means at one spot in time, and DIACHRONIC means at different points in time, you can turn SYNCHRONIC and DIACHRONIC into SPOT and ROVER to remind you which is which.

Language cannot be fully described apart from an account of the community that uses it **and** the effects of time. But the description cannot be accurate unless language as a SYSTEM is viewed **separately** from the effects of time on that system. So, Saussure divides linguistics into SYNCHRONIC and DIACHRONIC. A SYNCHRONIC STUDY examines the relations among co-existing elements of a language and is therefore independent of any time factor by definition. It gives an account of a **state** of the language SYSTEM. The notion of a system implies that, if the account is valid, it will present that state as a **whole** of interacting elements. By contrast, a DIACHRONIC STUDY describes an **evolution** in which only **fragments** of states of a language at different times are relevant to the account.

For the linguist, aiming at a complete description of a language, SYNCHRONIC and DIACHRONIC analysis have to go together; for a community of language speakers, SYNCHRONIC and DIACHRONIC facts do <u>not</u> come together. When a language system is put to use in speech or writing, only SYNCHRONIC elements come into play. Nobody needs to know the history of a language to be able to master its system. Moreover, DIACHRONIC facts do not alter the SYSTEM **as system**. To illustrate this point, Saussure offers an analogy: If one of the planets of our solar system changed weight and dimensions, those changes would disturb the equilibrium of the whole, but it would remain a whole.

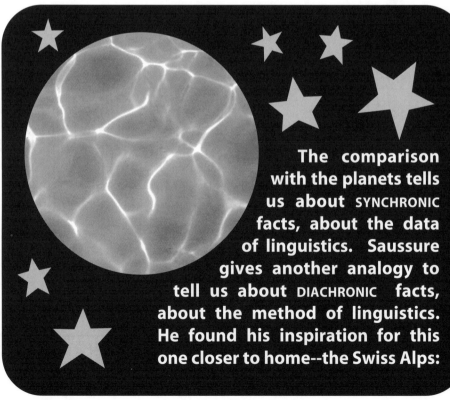

The comparison with the planets tells us about SYNCHRONIC facts, about the data of linguistics. Saussure gives another analogy to tell us about DIACHRONIC facts, about the method of linguistics. He found his inspiration for this one closer to home--the Swiss Alps:

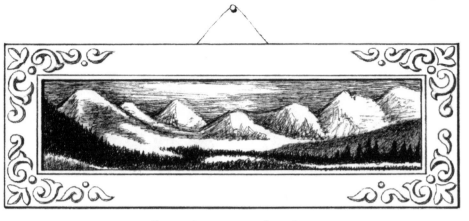

Synchronic Analysis

If an artist wants to paint a panorama of the mountains, she has to choose a fixed vantage point. Showing the scene from several peaks at once would be absurd, Saussure notes.

(Interestingly enough, cubism, with its multiple perspectives, began to develop at exactly the same time that Saussure taught his course on general linguistics; we don't know what he might have thought of cubism, but its principle can have no place in his synchronic linguistics.)

SYNCHRONIC ANALYSIS must be confined to one point of view in order to show the whole language system.

By contrast, a DIACHRONIC ANALYSIS traces the evolution of language, looking not at the whole system but at individual elements of it at different times.

In this case, the comparison can be made to an artist going from one mountain peak to another to note shifts in perspective. Recording these shifts does not give a panorama. In linguistics, the panorama belongs to SYNCHRONIC ANALYSIS.

Voilà!

Diachronic Analysis

♪ YNCHRONIC AND DIACHRONIC ARE <u>AUTONOMOUS</u> BUT <u>INTERDEPENDENT</u>

In linguistics, we don't learn the state of a language by studying the changes it has undergone. The study of the state is SYNCHRONIC analysis; the study of changes is DIACHRONIC analysis.

Using Saussure's favorite comparison, the functioning of language is like a game of chess. This is the best analogy, he says, because chess shows us a system of values. These differ for pawns, knights, etc., but together, all the pieces form a SYSTEM. They interact like elements of language in a SYNCHRONIC state. It's the interaction that creates their value. Any state of the chessboard during a game is comparable to a SYNCHRONIC state of language.

But when a piece is moved, the effect is like a linguistic change, and that's DIACHRONIC analysis. The move only involves one piece, but it has an effect on the whole system, just as we saw in the case of the solar system, just as it is in language. The chessboard is in one state before the move and another state after the move, but the move itself doesn't belong to either state. It's the same for language:

DIACHRONIC FACTS don't belong to a state of a language, because LANGUAGE STATES are SYNCHRONIC.

35

Saussure ends his lesson on the synchronic/diachronic duality by relating it to the language/speech duality this way:

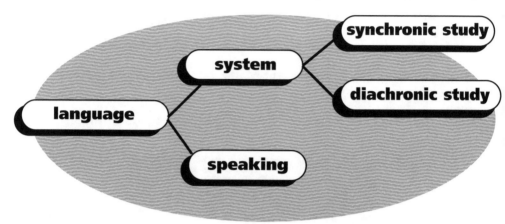

SYNCHRONIC LINGUISTICS deals with logical and psychological relations that <u>link</u> coexisting terms in a system; DIACHRONIC LINGUISTICS deals with terms that <u>replace</u> one another as a system evolves, **but which do not form a system themselves.** Saussure speaks of SYNCHRONIC and DIACHRONIC as the diverging paths that linguistics can take.

"Who's Chomsky?"

When Noam Chomsky started to develop transforma-tional genera-tive grammar in the 1950s, he said linguistics should be interested not only in **particular languages** but also in the **general nature of language**. Generative linguistics has gone through many phases, but its emphasis has always been on SYNCHRONIC analysis.

THE ELEMENTS OF LANGUAGE AS SYSTEM ARE <u>NOT</u> ABSTRACTIONS BUT CONCRETE ENTITIES

C.K. Ogden

T.A. Richards

Saussure

J.R. Firth

Ogden: Saussure does not pause to ask himself what he is look-ing for, or whe-ther there is any reason why there should be such a thing. He concocts a suitable object -- *la langue* -- as opposed to speech.

Richards: Inventing verbal entities outside the range of possible investigation proved fatal to the theory of SIGNS which followed.

Saussure: Not these two again!

J. R. Firth: There is no such thing as *la langue*.

Saussure : This could become an epidemic.

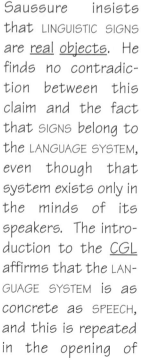

Saussure insists that LINGUISTIC SIGNS are <u>real</u> <u>objects</u>. He finds no contradiction between this claim and the fact that SIGNS belong to the LANGUAGE SYSTEM, even though that system exists only in the minds of its speakers. The introduction to the <u>CGL</u> affirms that the LANGUAGE SYSTEM is as concrete as SPEECH, and this is repeated in the opening of

Part II -- SYNCHRONIC LINGUISTICS. Let's look at Saussure's reasons for making this claim.

SIGNS can be made tangible through writing, whereas SPEECH, a continuum of movements involving lips, tongue, lungs, teeth, etc., cannot be so readily represented. Moreover, it is the SIGNIFIER-SIGNIFIED LINK that makes the SIGN concrete.

A sequence of sounds is not a LINGUISTIC ELEMENT unless it is linked to an IDEA. And an IDEA is not a LINGUISTIC ELEMENT unless it is paired with a SEQUENCE OF SOUNDS. This view shows us how the notion of the TWO-PART SIGN met Saussure's requirements for a starting point in developing the notion of LANGUAGE AS SYSTEM.

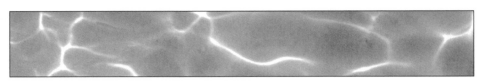

Saussure summarizes this last bit with another comparison: Water is composed of hydrogen and oxygen, but neither one of these has the properties of water. Neither the SIGNIFIER nor the SIG-NIFIED has the properties of the LINGUISTIC SIGN.

Saussure brings the principle of the LINEARITY of the SIGNIFIER back in to explain the difference between LINGUISTIC SIGNS and visual signs. Our eyes do the work of keeping the form of visual signs distinct from one another. With LINGUISTIC SIGNS, our minds have to do the work to separate one word from the next in the flow of speech, and this is where **meaning** comes in.

Speech is like a chain; that's why we say the SIGNIFIER is LINEAR. But we can't identify the links in the chain till we match meanings to their FORMS. Let's take the contrast between a pair of sentences as an example here:

WE CAN'T AIR IT OUT.
WE CAN TEAR IT OUT.

or...

cantalope   can't elope

39

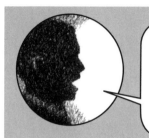

When we **look** at these examples, they are partly different; but say them out loud. The sequence of sounds is exactly the same in both.

It's easy to **see** the difference, but even when you **hear** them you put different meanings to them by making different divisions in the speech chain, breaking it up so that it contains different SIGNS. It is only when SIGNS are identified that the sound and meaning come together to form LINGUISTIC UNITS. But these units are not to be equated with words. If we go back to the definition of the SIGN, we see why not.

The SIGN is a LINK between a FORM that SIGNIFIES and a CONCEPT that is SIGNIFIED. That includes lots of words whose forms are simple, but there are just as many words whose forms are complex, so then there are SIGNS **within** the word.

Because so many words are complex, the word cannot be the basic unit of linguistic analysis.

Here is an example that we saw earlier. "Top" is a word, and it's also a SIGN. No complications here. "Tops" is a word, but it's **two** SIGNS. There's the SIGNIFIER "top" for the basic idea and the SIGNIFIER "s" to express the idea that there is more than one top.

Of the two SIGNS here, one is a word and one is not. Both are units, and that is why we can't take words as LINGUISTIC UNITS. There are bits of meaning within the word and chunks of meaning beyond the word.

Here are some more examples:

ONE WORD	NUMBER OF UNITS/SIGNS
mouse	1
mice	2
mouse-trap	2
mouse-traps	3
ox	1
oxen	2
a	1
an	1

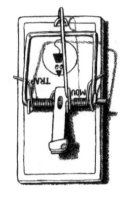

Going back to the comparison between language and chess, Saussure notes that just as the game consists entirely of the interaction of the pieces, language is a system based completely on oppositions between its concrete units. To be clear on what these units are, we need to understand the nature of IDENTITY and VALUE, as they apply to a SYNCHRONIC study.

CONTEXT AND CONTRAST CREATE SYNCHRONIC IDENTITY

When a LINK between FORM and MEANING recurs in two or more contexts (context = the background; the words before and after the word or "unit" in question), we take the recurring units to be identical. But this is not enough to establish IDENTITY, because elsewhere we take units to be identical even when their forms or meanings vary. So, for example, when we hear "Did you?" then "Did ya?" and finally "Didja?" we identify the same SIGN (*you*) in spite of the variations of pronunciation. When we read "adopt a child" and "adopt a stance," we identify the same SIGN (*adopt*) in spite of the obvious difference in MEANING.

Saussure finds more comparisons to bring the point home. If an express train leaves Geneva for Paris every evening, the locomotive, the coaches, and the personnel will not always be the same, but we think of it and refer to it as the same train. If all the buildings on a street are demolished and rebuilt, we will continue to think of it as the same street. **If I see the same jacket as mine, I do not think of it as identical,** because the jacket is a purely material entity, and obviously there are two of them. By contrast,

Same coat, different chick...

the express and the street are not purely material. The express takes part of its identity from being different from the local train, from an express that leaves in the morning, etc. The street takes part of its identity from its relation to other streets.

Same coat, different chick...

SYNCHRONIC IDENTITY IS SEPARABLE FROM SYNCHRONIC VALUE

I'm a knight.

I'm a knight, too.

I'm a knight in training!

Back to the chessboard. Let's take the knight. **Is its unique identity (its shape) an essential element of the game?** No. It's the position on the board and conditions of the game that are essential. If you can't find the knight when you're setting up the board to start a game, you can **replace it** by something of **any** shape--as long as the new piece makes only the moves the knight would have.

43

The key to this concept is remembering that the LINGUISTIC SIGN links SOUNDS and IDEAS. Without that link, it would be impossible to separate one thought from another. But sounds are no more distinct than unexpressed thoughts. The function of language is <u>not</u> to create a sound medium for the expression of thought but to mediate **between** thought and sound, so that the link between them will result in mutually determined units.

Thought, which is chaotic by nature, acquires order when it acquires form.

I can't resist another comparison: When air is in contact with a body of water, and the air pressure changes, the surface of the water breaks up into waves. The waves are like the coming together of thought and sound in the linguistic sign.

It is like the wave upon the water.

Saussure also offers the comparison between the LINGUISTIC SIGN and a sheet of paper. It is impossible to cut one side without cutting the other. The sound and the thought that are linked in a SIGN are just as inseparable as the two sides of the paper.

THE LINK BETWEEN SOUND AND THOUGHT IN THE LINGUISTIC SIGN PRODUCES FORM, NOT SUBSTANCE.

This notion brings us back to the arbitrariness of the SIGN and takes us forward to the idea of linguistic VALUE.

If the SIGN were not arbitrary, the SIGNS that make up language would not be **mutually** determined but **externally** determined. But LINGUISTIC VALUE **is** determined entirely by the existence of <u>relations</u>, and the SIGN must therefore be arbitrary. Saussure calls the relation between the SIGNIFIER and the SIGNIFIED and the relation between SIGNS "pure form", as a reminder that it consists of nothing but a <u>relation</u>.

MEANING IS DISTINCT FROM LINGUISTIC VALUE

Saussure distinguishes two types of MEANING: one belongs to the SIGN, to a SIGN taken individually; the other arises from the <u>contrast</u> between SIGNS. Meaning that is part of the SIGN is subordinate to meaning determined by contrast (contrast = to compare side by side, two things that are drastically different—like night and day), and so Saussure calls the latter **LINGUISTIC VALUE**, as a reminder of the difference.

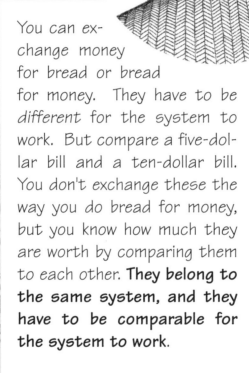

There is a paradox in the principle for any system of VALUES. The system must consist of 1) something **unlike** whatever it can be **exchanged for**, the VALUE of which is to be determined; 2) things **similar** to the one for which the VALUE is to be determined.

You can exchange money for bread or bread for money. They have to be different for the system to work. But compare a five-dollar bill and a ten-dollar bill. You don't exchange these the way you do bread for money, but you know how much they are worth by comparing them to each other. **They belong to the same system, and they have to be comparable for the system to work.**

You know how much a $5 bill and a £5 note are worth by comparing them to each other too. **They belong to <u>different</u> systems, but they have to be comparable for their systems to work.**

Sounds and ideas are like the bread and the money. If you are a baker, there is no point in exchanging your bread with another baker. If you are hungry, there is no point in exchanging your money for somebody else's. If you have an idea to get across, you can't do it with another idea. Ideas have to be exchanged for sounds, and sounds have to be exchanged for ideas, if speakers are to communicate MEANING.

But in addition to this type of meaning, the SIGN communicates LINGUISTIC VALUE, and this comes from its contrast with other SIGNS to which it is related (like the contrast between the $5 and the $10). Take the words ocean, lake, river, creek. Together they determine each other's meanings. Each term is understood partly because we know how it is different from each and all of the others. Ocean means what lake, river, creek do not; lake means what ocean, river, creek do not, etc

" yes, we have no bananas . . ."

The principle that distinguishes Value from Meaning distinguishes Forms from each other and creates Meaning.

Lake also means what it means because it is <u>different</u> <u>from</u> bake, fake, make, etc. These are <u>not</u> examples of related but contrasting meanings like lake, ocean, river, etc. that Saussure calls linguistic value; they <u>are</u> examples of contrasting <u>forms</u>. There is a minimal difference of one sound at the beginning of each word in the group lake, bake, take, fake. That is enough to make each of them a signifier of a different sign. The minimal difference in form allows a difference in meaning for each word.

Contrasts are not limited to this type. It is enough for a sound to be present in one word and absent in another for a difference in meaning to be created: ache and lake, ocean and motion, reek and creek. These are also minimal pairs, just like lake and bake, etc.

I'm not a goose, I'm a moose!

I'm not a moose, I'm a goose!

Note to the Mystified Reader:

No matter how clear one tries to make Saussure's marvellous ideas, some readers—perhaps even most readers—will, at some point, be cross-eyedcrosseyed with confusion, overdosed on abstruse abstractions...and wondering if or not they are "getting it."

Let me assure that you are getting it—or to be a bit more forthcoming, that you will get it if you keep on keeping on, for these reasons: Saussure's ideas are "circular." They're like a good mystery movie: Only when you get to the end, do you fullyfullly understand the beginning. Some of Saussure's ideas may strike you as so abstract and nit-picky that nobody could actually use them...so you will be slightly amazed by exactly how Saussure's theories were used to transform not only linguistics, but anthropology, psychology, philosophy, and even literary criticism—and amazingly amazed that you will understand those changes.

Just keep the faith.

$\mathcal{L}$INGUSTIC FORMS ARE <u>CONTRASTIVE</u>, <u>RELATIVE</u>, AND <u>NEGATIVE</u> ENTITIES

Minimal pairs (like *did you, did ya*) show us how linguistic forms function to give meaning by <u>contrasting</u> with each other. Since SIGNS belong to the LANGUAGE SYSTEM and not to SPEECH, these forms (or SIGNIFIERS) do not consist of sounds. (Sounds only occur in speech.) A LINGUISTIC FORM has <u>no</u> substance, <u>no</u> presence, <u>no</u> positive qualities to give it substance or presence. It consists of the <u>differences</u> that separate it from all other forms. The language SYSTEM requires only differences.

Let's go back to our example of *did you, did ya, didja*. These variations in pronunciation don't affect communication. Any one of them contrasts with *did he, did we, etc.* There is no confusion of meaning, as long as there is a <u>difference</u> of <u>form</u>. If *did he* is shortened to *"didee"*, it still contrasts with *did we*. But *did he* and *did we* can't both be shortened to *"didee"* or else the contrast in meaning is lost.

$\mathcal{I}$N THE LANGUAGE SYSTEM, THERE ARE ONLY <u>DIFFERENCES</u>

In general, the concept of difference implies **positive terms between which the difference exists,** but in **the language system** this is not so.

Meaning is carried by differences alone.

No positive terms are required for the formation of a system, which functions to create differences among ideas and differences among sound-images. When we analyze these differences in SIGNIFIERS and SIGNIFIEDS taken separately, they are pure difference, pure form, purely negative. But from the point of view of the SIGN, where SIGNIFIER and SIGNIFIED come together, we are no longer dealing with a negative element.

*I*N THE LANGUAGE SYSTEM, THERE ARE ONLY <u>DIFFERENCES</u>

A SIGN's form differs from that of other SIGNS as form; a SIGN's concept differs from that of other SIGNS as concept. But as a SIGN it does not **differ** from others; it is merely **distinct** from them. (The difference between "*differ* from" and "*distinct* from" is subtle: a *difference* is something you can define by using a third term [the *difference* between A and B is C]; to be *distinct* from is a simple assertion that A is *not identical to* B.) Every feature of language structure that Saussure develops from this point forward is based on the distinctiveness of the SIGN, the **oppositions** among SIGNS. There is even a basic opposition of types of relations among SIGNS in SYNCHRONIC linguistics:

<u>LINEAR</u> <u>RELATIONS</u> are complex signs, sign-sequences with two or more components: *mouse-trap* (2), *mouse-traps* (3), *the mouse-traps* (4), *set the m o u s e - traps* (5), etc. (<u>Linear</u> = arranged in an orderly line or meaningful sequence) <u>NON-LIN-EAR</u> <u>RELATIONS</u> are associ- ations of form or meaning, or both, that language-users automatically make for any sign: *mouse/mice*, *mouse/rat*, *mouse/house*, *trap/trap-ping/trapped*, *trap/catch*, *trap/snap, mouse-trap/rat-trap, etc.*

*L*INEAR RELATIONS BELONG TO THE <u>LANGUAGE</u> <u>SYSTEM</u>

Speech is linear, and so LINEAR RELATIONS *might seem to belong to speech. But they do not, because the type of* LINEAR RELA-TIONS *Saussure is defining here are* SIGN-SEQUENCES, *and* SIGNS *belong only to the language* SYSTEM, *not to speech.*

Saussure distinguishes between LINEAR RELATIONS that are <u>fixed</u> and those that are <u>free</u>. The expression *have a cold* is <u>fixed</u>; we cannot get the same meaning across by substituting *be with a cold*, *have coldness,* or any other phrase we might try to invent.

And *have a cold* is not a PATTERN for other expressions; we cannot say *have a hot, have a warm, have a cool.* By contrast, *a cold day* is a <u>free</u> expression with the same pattern as many others: *a hot day, a warm day, a cool day, a cold month, a cold season,* etc. *Have a cold* is a LINEAR SIGN-SEQUENCE of the type Saussure defines for purposes of showing how such sequences interact with associations among SIGNS.

ASSOCIATIONS AMONG <u>SIGNS</u> BELONG TO THE LANGUAGE SYSTEM

Language-users make connections among SIGNS on the basis of SIGNIFIERS or SIGNIFIEDS, or both. Any word, says Saussure, is like the center of a constellation of associations.

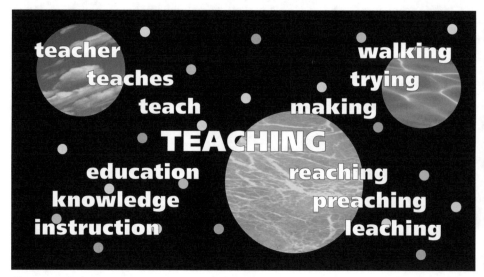

teacher
teaches
teach
walking
trying
making
TEACHING
education
knowledge
instruction
reaching
preaching
leaching

These word-groups are never spoken as groups, because they belong to the language SYSTEM, not to speech.

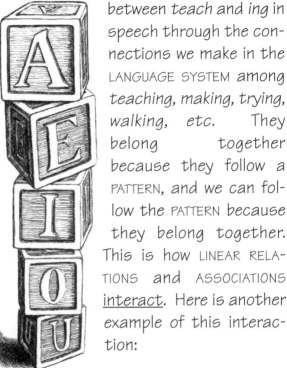

Teaching is used as an example here because it has a LINEAR RELATION in it. But just because it is linear doesn't mean it's *teach + ing*. *Ing* is never used by itself, so it is not simply added to *teach* the way we would add a word to make a grammatical structure like *teach math*. We make the connection between *teach* and *ing* in speech through the connections we make in the LANGUAGE SYSTEM among *teaching, making, trying, walking*, etc. They belong together because they follow a PATTERN, and we can follow the PATTERN because they belong together. This is how LINEAR RELATIONS and ASSOCIATIONS <u>interact</u>. Here is another example of this interaction:

> ## UNCOVER
> **unbend**
> **unscramble**
> **etc.**
>
> **recover**
> **discover**
> **etc.**

Uncover is a complex **SIGN** with an **INTERNAL LINEAR RELATION**. It functions as a **UNIT** because it belongs to two groups of the **NONLINEAR RELATIONS** we call **ASSOCIATIONS**.

A COMPLEX SIGN WITH AN INTERNAL LINEAR RELATION IS <u>NOT</u> COMPLETELY ARBITRARY

Why is a bird called a bird? No reason, really. It's called *un oiseau* in French and *ein Vogel* in German. The sign is **arbitrary**. Why is a bird-cage called a bird-cage? Because it's a cage for a bird. Is the SIGN **arbitrary** in this case? No. *Bird* is a SIMPLE SIGN and arbitrary; *cage* is a SIMPLE SIGN and arbitrary. But *bird-cage* is a COMPLEX SIGN and not arbitrary. We understand the relation between the SIGNIFIER and the SIGNIFIED of the COMPLEX SIGN as a whole because we recognize the relation between its parts. When this happens, the SIGN is *not* arbitrary; it is <u>MOTIVATED.</u>

When a complex sign is <u>motivated</u> by its parts, it belongs to groups of ASSOCIATED words of the type shown above for *uncover:* 1) uncover, unbend, unscramble; 2) uncover, recover, discover. Another example would be *besinger, grower, user talker, etc.,* where we recognize a PATTERN OF MEANING--a person who does the action indicated by the first part of the word. In this case, there are other words that appear to follow the same pattern but do not: *sweater, slipper, stapler, facer, etc.* They belong to a series of associations where FORM is similar, but there is no connection in MEANING--as in *teaching, reaching, preaching.*

The principles that Saussure calls **LINGUISTIC VALUE** and **OPPOSITIONS** distinguish signs from each other; **LINEAR RELATIONS** in the SIGN and **ASSOCIATIONS** among SIGNS bind them together. It is this binding together that limits the arbitrariness of the LINGUISTIC SIGN--the principle with which Saussure opened his teaching. When arbitrariness is limited, the SIGN is said to be **MOTIVATED**. If the SIGNS of language were completely arbitrary, they would be much more difficult to learn. All

languages limit the arbitrariness of their SIGNS to some degrees, and Saussure sees in this variation a basis for the classification of languages.

If we didn't have compound words like *bird-cage* in English, we would have to learn *bird* and *cage* and a third word instead of just combining them. For counting from *1-100*, we would need a hundred separate words, instead, we have just 28: simple and ARBITRARY (UNMOTIVATED) SIGNS like *one, two, three* and MOTIVATED combinations like *twenty-one, twenty-two, etc.*

ASSOCIATIONS AMONG SIGNS AND INEAR RELATIONS IN THE SIGN FORM THE BASIS OF THE GRAMMATICAL SYSTEM

The users of a language not only know automatically what associations belong to a given word, they know what distinguishes various types of associations from each other. The link among *teaching, teach, teaches, etc.* is different from that of *teaching, making, trying, etc.* Being clear on that difference is the link between knowledge of word-associations and knowledge of grammar.

ASSOCIATIONS like *teaching, education, instruction, etc.* are based on MEANING alone, without the extra link of RECURRING SIGNIFIERS as in *teaching/teach, teaching/making.*

This is why I believe that progressively wider ASSOCIATIONS form the basis of our knowledge of grammatical categories--nouns, adjectives, verbs, etc.

I want him to tell the truth

We have moved here from connections among specific words to the categories of grammar, from concrete entities to abstract ones. (An <u>abstraction</u> = presents the qualities of something, but <u>not</u> the thing itself; its opposite is a <u>concrete object</u>.) There can be no abstractions in grammar without concrete elements to serve as their basis. The same is true when we move from ASSOCIATIONS to LINEAR RELATIONS. Word order is an abstraction, but there can be no word order without the concrete presence of words. How could we speak of a contrast in word order creating a difference in meaning unless we took examples? *(see right)*

I want to tell him the truth

Meaning and grammatical function exist only with the help of specific forms.

DIACHRONIC LINGUISTICS

In the lessons on **SYNCHRONIC ANALYSIS**, Saussure taught that the **LINGUISTIC SIGN** is both changeable and unchangeable. Because of the **SIGN**'s changeable quality, a **DIACHRONIC** approach to linguistics is both possible and necessary, if the subject is to be completely covered.

The evolution of sounds is incompatible with the notion of a language **SYSTEM**, which is what **SYNCHRONIC** linguistics studies, so tracing the evolution of sounds comes under the separate heading of **DIACHRONIC LINGUISTICS**.

PHONETIC CHANGES ARE COMPLETELY REGULAR

SYNCHRONIC ANALYSIS begins with the concept of the LINGUISTIC SIGN; DIACHRONIC ANALYSIS does not need to begin here, because the changes that it studies do not affect the SIGN **as sign**.

Modern English *mouse, louse, house* used to be pronounced like "moose," "loose," and "hoose" in Old English. When the change in pronunciation—a PHONETIC CHANGE—occurred, it affected all of them in the same way. As SIGNS, they continued to be used in the same way, with the same LINGUISTIC VALUE, though their pronunciation had changed.

59

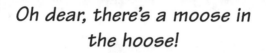

> *Oh dear, there's a moose in the hoose!*

PHONETIC CHANGES ARE <u>CONDITIONED</u> BY <u>CONTEXT</u>

Even though PHONETIC CHANGES are completely regular, they rarely affect every word in the language that contains the sound undergoing change.

As Latin developed, s between vowels shifted to r (*gensis*,  became *generis*, *asena* became *arena*), but in other positions s remained s.

PHONETIC CHANGES MAY BE <u>IMMEDIATE</u> OR <u>MEDIATED</u>

The shift from *genesis* and *asena* to *generis* and *arena* did not occur as a simple, one-stage operation. This would be impossible, because s and r do not share the right features to allow such a change. First s changed to z, a minimal change involving only the addition of vibration of the vocal cords as the sound of s is produced.

60

Then, when z was eliminated from the sound system of Latin, it was replaced by the closely related r. This is an example of a MEDIATED PHONETIC CHANGE.

NOT ALL "CAUSES" OF PHONETIC CHANGE DESERVE THE NAME

Saussure rejects the notion, traditionally held in his day, that race PREDISPOSES PHONETIC CHANGES. Would it be correct to say that the "Latin mouth" favored the shift from s to r in the examples given above? Certainly not, because some time after the shift was complete, s was reintroduced into Latin and is once again found between vowels in some words. It is only correct, at most, to say that at a given moment there is general tendency for a certain PHONETIC CHANGE to occur in a certain context in a given language. (Whew!)

PHONETIC CHANGES have been explained as part of a process of adaptation

to geography and climate. In this regard, it has been pointed out that the languages of northern Europe favor consonants and those of the south favor vowels. But while it is true that the Scandinavian languages follow this pattern, it is also true

that Finnish and Lappish have more vowels than Italian. And certain dialects of southern France are marked by more consonant clusters than their northern counterparts. Part of the geography-and-climate fallacy is in thinking and speaking of a tendency without taking a time frame into consideration. The consonant clusters of German are only a relatively recent phenomenon, dating from the period when the language lost its final vowels after accented syllables.

The principle-of-least-effort applied to language says that a group of sounds will be reduced to one, that a sound requiring forceful articulation will be replaced by one requiring less force, that final syllables will tend to be dropped, etc. This seems at first to be an explanation for phonetic change which is superior to that of race and geography. But here again there are counter-examples-- cases where German, Spanish, and other languages have undergone phonetic changes where the new sounds require greater effort of articulation than those they have replaced. In fact, as Saussure observes, there is no way to determine with certainty what a given language will consider to be an easy or difficult element of pronunciation. Physiological and psychological factors interact to decide this.

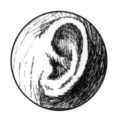   

Another view is that language acquisition, with its trial and error, plants the seed for phonetic change. Errors which go uncorrected in a child's speech eventually form part of the standard language of that child's generation. But, Saussure notes, there are common errors in children's speech which have never taken

root in the language system. Moreover, all such errors are spontaneous and equal, which leaves no explanation for why some

should produce an effect on the system and others not. (This applies to the so-called factors of race, geography, and the principle of least effort as well.)

Historical reasons for language change, particularly social and political

upheaval, have been proposed. The most frequently cited example is that of Latin undergoing major changes in its development into the Romance languages at the time when the Roman Empire was enduring many invasions. Saussure offers two cautions in this regard. 1) Political stability and political instability exert different types of influence on language--the former in a positive way by allowing external factors such as a royal court, a school, an academy, or literature to affect the language; the latter in a negative way by

diminishing or eliminating such external factors and

allowing language to develop freely. 2) While grammar, being linked to thought, is susceptible to changes in periods of upheaval, there is no evidence that such

periods favor an increased rate of PHONETIC CHANGE. Conversely, even stable periods of history show language undergoing PHONETIC CHANGE.

According to another hypothesis, PHONETIC CHANGE may be explained by the presence of a native people whose language has been displaced by that of newcomers. The native language then exerts its influence on the other. Saussure points out that such circumstances have occurred only rarely and that their analysis is not free of the obscurities already noted in relation to questions of race, geography, etc.

Bonjour!

Howdy!

The final notion regarding PHONETIC CHANGE that Saussure discusses is, he says, no explanation at all but simply an analogy to

changes of fashion. About these we can know nothing more than that they depend on imitation. But even though this notion carries no power of explanation, Saussure mentions it because it has the advantage of setting PHONETIC CHANGE in a larger context and giving it a psychological basis. It forces the linguist to ask: "Where is the starting point of imitation?"

$\mathscr{P}$HONETIC CHANGE HAS <u>NO</u> LIMITS

Saussure's lessons here under the heading of DIACHRON-IC LINGUISTICS are related to what he taught about SYN-CHRONIC LINGUISTICS. There is a connec-tion with his very first lesson: nothing imposes limits on PHONETIC CHANGE, and the reason for this is the ARBITRARINESS of the LINGUISTIC SIGN. How far a process of PHONETIC CHANGE will con-tinue is unpre-dictable,

because the SIGNIFI-ER of a SIGN could go on changing indefi-nitely, and the SIGN would still function as a SIGN.

Not only is the extent of a PHO-NETIC CHANGE unpre-dictable, it affects all parts of speech equally. If it were confined to nouns or adjective or verbs, the change, which is DIACHRONIC, would

be conditioned by SYNCHRONIC FACTS, and that is impossible.

$\mathscr{P}$HONETIC CHANGE <u>ALTERS</u> SYNCHRONIC FACTS

Let's take a look at some interesting words that will show us the effect of PHONETIC CHANGE.

Delicious and delight. Do we make a connection between these words? Perhaps, because something that is delicious is a delight. But what about these pairs:

bitter	bite
doctor	docile
vacant	vacation
specimen	speculate

Most speakers of English would not connect the meanings of these words, but just like *delicious-delight*, they come from the same root word in Latin or Old English. In each pair, the parts of speech to which the words belong is different, so there was a grammatical difference between them to begin with. But as PHONETIC CHANGE was added to that difference, it ensured that the connection between the words would be lost. In Latin, *berbicarius* was derived from *berbix* (shepherd from sheep), but in French these became *berger*
66

and *brebis*. Here the connection of FORM is even weaker than for English *sheep-shepherd*, and so the SIGNIFIERS do not support a connection between the CONCEPTS SIGNIFIED. The proof of this weakened link is that, in some variants of French, *berger* can mean *cattle-herder*. The link with *sheep* is completed severed. The connection between *Venus* and *venereal* has also been lost, but for more complicated reasons.

We are looking at examples here of DIACHRONIC CHANGE, but the results show the effect of such changes on LINGUISTIC VALUE, which is a SYNCHRONIC feature of language. Now let's take a case that contrasts with the word-pairs on the preceeding page:

gorge-gorgeous

Here there has been no PHONETIC CHANGE to obscure the link between two words from the same root, but most speakers would not associate them. You don't have to know word-histories (etymology) to use a language system, but you do have to know them to make a connection between *gorge* and *gorgeous*. That's why Saussure said:

ETYMOLOGY* and SYNCHRONIC VALUE are two different things.

(<u>Etymology</u> = The origin and historical development of words.)

PHONETIC CHANGE can occur without a link in meaning being lost. The prefix for the idea of "not" has developed several forms in English, all of which speakers understand and associate with each other:

*in*direct, *im*possible,
*ir*relevant, *il*legal.

The INTERNAL STRUCTURE of complex words can disappear as a result of the PHONETIC CHANGE they undergo. *Neighbor* comes from Old English *neahgebur*, a compound form consisting of the words for *near* and *dweller*. *Lord* derives from *hlafweard*, a compound of the words for *loaf* and *keeper*. PHONETIC CHANGE has eroded these words so much that they have lost their recognizable component parts.

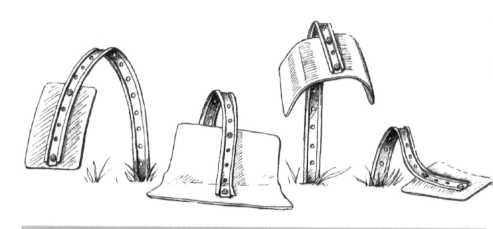

Since they are no longer COMPLEX SIGNS, as they were in Old English, they have also lost their MOTIVATION.

There are also words where little or no PHONETIC CHANGE has taken place, but we do not recognize them as previously COMPLEX SIGNS, unless we know their history: *atone* comes from the phrase *at one*. Again there is loss of MOTIVATION,

even without the effect of radical PHONETIC CHANGE.

Saussure teaches that there are no PHONETIC DOUBLETS--no cases where a single word has evolved two different forms. It is incorrect, for example to think of *feed* and *fed* or *meet* and *met* as variants of the same form. In Old English, long vow-

els were usually shortened before double consonants. The vowel contrasts for our examples in modern English were already present at that stage of the language's development in *fedan/fedde*, *metan/mette*.

Where alternations of sound occur in related forms with some regularity or recognizable pattern, it is customary to think of them as grammatical rules. Saussure points out that such rules are only the chance result of PHONETIC CHANGE--cases where the LANGUAGE SYSTEM has assigned differences of MEANING to differences of FORM. So, for example, the patterns of variation in lead/led, bleed/bled, sing/sang, ring/rang began as phonetic changes which English came to use to indicate the difference between present tense and past tense.

Saussure made the point when introducing the SYNCHRONIC/ DIACHRONIC distinction that a DIACHRONIC FACT is an autonomous event. Particular SYNCHRONIC consequences that may result from it are completely unrelated to it. SYNCHRONIC FACTS are so similar to DIACHRONIC FACTS that they are confused.

Some linguists even think it is pointless to separate them. But if we do not, it is impossible to get a full and accurate picture of the history of a language, or an explanation of how language functions as a SYSTEM.

THE PROCESS OF ANALOGY <u>COUNTERBALANCES</u> PHONETIC CHANGE

Between them, PHONETIC CHANGE and the PROCESS OF ANALOGY account for all modifi-

"If the past tense of sing is sung, then bring is brung...") ANALOGY presupposes

and most common way of forming the plural of a noun in English is to add s.

cations in the FORM of the LINGUISTIC SIGN. (<u>Analogy</u> = In general usage, it is an extended comparison between two things that are not not usually paired ["A woman is like a tree, Grasshopper..."]; in linguistics, it is the process of inferring,

a PATTERN which is regularly imitated. An ANALOGICAL FORM is constructed on the model of one or more other forms according to a specific rule. ANALOGY generalizes the way in which a grammatical element is formed. So, for example, the regular

Irregular plurals have been eliminated by analogy to this model: in Old English the plural of cow was kine, but this was eliminated in favor or cows.

70

In his discussion of analogy Saussure gives his most explicit criticism of earlier approaches to linguistics. He notes that ANALOGY had been called

false analogy

in the belief that any divergence from a given order of linguistic facts was an irregularity and a departure from an ideal form. A state of language, arbitrarily taken as original, was assumed to be superior and correct, with no thought that it could itself contain irregularities and be a departure from a still earlier state.

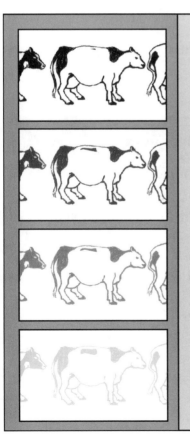

This observation already contains a hint to answering a question that Saussure raises: *Is it correct to think of ANALOGY as PHONETIC CHANGE?* ANALOGY is always a process involving three elements: a <u>form</u> which is <u>affected</u>, one or more <u>forms</u> to serve as a <u>model</u> for the analogy, and a <u>new form</u> resulting from the process. But the affected form is not part of the process, because this consists of the model or models being extended to produce a new form. In the case of cow/kine, the models that affect the disappearance of the irregular plural are all the regular plurals formed by the addition of *s*, and in particular those with a singular resembling *cow: sow/sows, plow/plows, bow/bows.*

When *cows* came into being on the ANALOGY to this series, there was an initial period when both *kine* and *cows* were in use. Gradually *kine* disappeared and was **replaced** by *cows*. There was no process of transformation from *kine* to *cows*. The proof of this is that there are no other examples of PHONETIC CHANGE from *-ine* to *-ows*.

In any case where there is replacement of an opposition of the type *cow/kine: cow/cows*, there is a tendency to identify the corresponding terms and to assume that the original has been modified. This is contrary to fact and to the laws of sound change. Let's look at another example: At one time *laughter* was pronounced like *daughter*

and *slaughter*. The pronunciation changed on the analogy to *laugh*. This could not be a PHONETIC SHIFT. If it were, there would have to be a rule that created the sound of *f* out of nothing, which is impossible. And if it

Loff, loff, loff!

were possible, the pronunciation of *daughter* and *slaughter* would have changed too. The PROCESS OF ANALOGY is one of <u>replacement</u>, not phonetic change.

A NALOGY IS A <u>CREATIVE</u> FORCE IN LANGUAGE

ANALOGY

PHONETIC CHANGE

Saussure calls ANALOGY a grammatical feature of language. *(REMINDER: For Saussure, ASSOCIATIONS among SIGNS and LINEAR RELATIONS in the SIGN form the basis of the grammatical system.)* For ANALOGY to operate, speakers must understand and be aware of the relations between forms. Meaning comes into play. Here is a contrast between ANALOGY and PHONETIC CHANGE, because the latter takes place independently of meaning. But new forms created through ANALOGY could have no basis, if speakers did not LINK FORMS through MEANING.

In the discussion of ANALOGY, the *Course in General Linguistics* is at its most explicit about the connections among its principles. **Three main points are raised:**

1) ANALOGY shows the necessity of a linguistic analysis where the LANGUAGE SYSTEM is treated separately from SPEECH;

2) it also shows that SPEECH depends on the LANGUAGE SYSTEM, and that the latter consists of the interaction of the LINEAR and ASSOCIATIVE relations set out in the lessons on SYNCHRONIC linguistics;

3) because it is grammatical and SYNCHRONIC, ANALOGY confirms Saussure's concept of an opposition between the ARBITRARINESS of SIMPLE LINGUISTIC SIGNS and the MOTIVATION OF COMPLEX ONES. SIMPLE SIGNS are never the basis for ANALOGICAL creation.

ANALOGY is part of how language works. That makes it part of language as a SYSTEM. That makes it part of SYNCHRONIC LINGUISTICS. But ANALOGY gives results that must be studied as part of DIACHRONIC analysis.

All linguistic change starts with one speaker using a new form like *cows* instead of *kine*, *gived* instead of *gave*, or *doed* instead of *did*. As children learn to speak, they keep trying out innovations such as *gived* and *doed*. If a new form is imitated and repeated by enough speakers, it gradually takes the place of the older one in the language system, the way *cows* replaced *kine*. Sometimes it is a process of reconstructing the elements of the system, as in the examples above. Sometimes it is a matter of reidentifying and reinterpreting existing terms. In both cases, the result is the creation of new forms by ANALOGY.

Forms

For Saussure, the process of ANALOGY begins with the interaction of FORM and MEANING. The general tendency of ANALOGY is to replace older, irregular forms by regular ones to create COMPLEX SIGNS made up of recognizable parts that can be found in other complex signs.

Forms

74

This type of ANALOGICAL CREATION *(cows, gived, doed)* turns ARBITRARY SIGNS into MOTIVATED SIGNS. The PROCESS OF ANALOGY can begin and develop because of the ARBITRARINESS of the LINGUISTIC SIGN, but the product is the MOTIVATION of the SIGN.

A NALOGY IS A STRONGER FORCE IN THE EVOLUTION OF LANGUAGE THAN PHONETIC CHANGE

ANALOGY does not so much change the elements of language as redistribute them. Here is Saussure's ANALOGY for analogy: Language is a garment covered with patches cut from its own cloth. When *kine* got torn out of English, the plural of cow got patched with the *s* that was already there for all the regular plurals. For this reason, even though ANALOGY involves creation and replacement of forms, we can say that it is a conservative force.

ANALOGY is also conservative because it stabilizes SIGNS and UNIFIES them in groups that have exactly the same basis as the

groups of ASSOCIATIONS we saw earlier. *Cows, plows, sows, bows, etc.* is an example. This group is just a part of the huge number of nouns that show the plural by adding s to their sin- g u l a r f o r m .

ANALOGY d r e w c o w s into this SERIES OF FORMS, and ANALOGY protects the series from undergoing any changes. A LINGUISTIC SIGN is much less susceptible to change when its SIGNIFIER is partly the same as that of

another SIGN, and there is a grammatical connection between them, such as plural for the example here.

If a word is complex in structure, language-users perceive it both as a whole and as a LINEAR RELATION. It is maintained so long as its elements are maintained. If a word is neither complex in structure nor easily linked to a series of other words (by form or meaning or both), it is free of the pressures that can lead to replacement by ANALOGY.

A N A L O G Y

Here we see two para-doxes: Linguistic change through ANALOGY is caused by ASSOCIATIONS and prevented by them; resistance to linguistic change through ANALOGY is caused by ASSOCIATIONS and the absence of them.

Because ANALOGY is so widespread, and because it involves the SIGN (its parts, its interpretation, and its qualities), it is much more powerful than PHONETIC CHANGE in the evolution of language that is the subject of DIACHRONIC ANALYSIS.

*A*NALOGY AND FOLK ETYMOLOGY OPERATE THROUGH MEANING

When part of a word suggests another one, the part can take over the whole, especially when the meaning of the part is clear, but the meaning of the whole is not. This is called FOLK ETYMOLOGY or POPULAR ETYMOLOGY. Middle English *agnail*, meaning a painful fingernail, mystified speakers with its *ag-*. As a result, it was transformed into *hangnail*. The process is quite common when foreign words are imported into a language.

Zut, alors! A picture of a crevice!

Speakers cannot resist the temptation to make the words over to conform to the patterns and models of their our language. **French _crevice_ became _crayfish_ in English.** _Cariole,_ a name for a type of horse-drawn carriage, became _carryall._ When the French borrowed _country dance,_ it turned into _contredanse_ (literally a _counter-dance_). All these changes involve MEANING, a reaction against the ARBITRARINESS of the SIGN, and the creation of a complex sign.

> _Oops! It's a **crayfish!**_

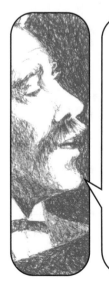

It would seem that FOLK ETYMOLOGY and ANALOGY are closely related, but Saussure emphasizes the differences between them.

> **_When ANALOGY occurs, an older form must be forgotten before the process concludes with the complete replacement of that form by the ANALOGICAL CREATION. For FOLK ETYMOLOGY, remembering the older form is the starting point for the change it undergoes._**

And this change involves analysis of the older form, which is never so in the case of ANALOGY. FOLK ETYMOLOGY involves only rare, technical, or borrowed words that trouble the understanding of language-users, but there are no restrictions on where ANALOGY occurs. It is widespread and part of the normal functioning of language, whereas FOLK ETYMOLOGY is exceptional.

*A*S LANGUAGE EVOLVES, SOME WORDS GET WELDED TOGETHER

Here we are looking at AGGLUTINATION—the linguistic process where separate words used in combination have turned into one word. Some of these are easy to recognize: *grownup, darkroom, fogbound,* **forget-me-not,** *nevertheless.*

Others are harder to spot, even when the spelling and pronunciation of the components have not changed very much: *holidays <holy days, breakfast <break fast.* The hardest ones to recognize are those where the component words are no longer used by themselves, or have changed too much in

spelling and meaning to give us any clue: *wardrobe, twilight, midriff, bellwether*.

Saussure stresses the contrast between AGGLUTINATION and ANALOGY, as he did between FOLK ETYMOLOGY and ANALOGY. AGGLUTINATION combines words which are otherwise independent, whereas ANALOGY operates below the level of the word on prefixes, roots, and suffixes. AGGLUTINATION takes place at the level of LINEAR RELATIONS among the words it combines, but ANALOGY involves both LINEAR RELATIONS and GROUPS OF ASSOCIATED WORDS. AGGLUTINATION is a simple and spontaneous procedure, in contrast to ANALOGY, where the process is initiated by reflection, analysis, and the intent to modify the language.

Diachronic Units and Identities Must Be Defined to Complete the Study of Linguistics

As Saussure concludes his lessons on DIACHRONIC LINGUISTICS, he relates them to his earlier teaching about SYNCHRONIC PHENOMENA. He writes that when the SIGN changes there is a shift in the relationship between the SIGNIFIER and the SIGNIFIED. This holds true not only for changes in the elements of a SIGN system but also for changes to the SYSTEM itself. The whole of the DIACHRONIC PHENOMENON is exactly this and nothing more.

To make the study of linguistics complete and consistent with his lessons on SYNCHRONIC ANALYSIS, Saussure raises the issue of DIACHRONIC UNITS. These are determined by asking a basic question: What element has been subjected directly to change?

How do we know the basis for stating that a linguistic element taken from one period is the same as an element taken from another period?

The problem that becomes apparent here is that the PHONETIC CORRESPONDENCES accounted for by the laws of regular sound change are not enough to account for IDENTITY.

Why not?

Because these correspondences are taken as evidence for the changes. They define the nature of the change, not the IDENTITY of what has changed.

HOW THE <u>GOAL</u> OF DIACHRONIC LINGUISTICS IS DEFINED

The only viewpoint in SYNCHRONIC ANALYSIS is that of language-users. In DIACHRONIC analysis, there are two possibilities: A linguistic change can be traced over the time period during which it occurred, but the linguist may also work back from result through cause to source. Because the historical evidence for language change is so often lacking, the linguist is forced into the second approach. And so the goal of DIACHRONIC LINGUIS-TICS becomes the reconstruction of older forms of language. It is detective work, where the more new forms there are to compare with older ones, the better the guess as to which ones are connected and how.

A LANGUAGE MAY BE OLDER THAN ANOTHER IN DIFFERENT WAYS

(Language can trap the linguist)

Saussure warns of a trap in the seemingly innocent phrase "older ones," when applied to language. There are no generations of language, as there are of human beings, because it continues to be spoken even as it develops and changes.

It is also necessary to distinguish between an "older" language state that is earlier in time and one which is more archaic-- closer in form to an original model. In the latter case, a language has undergone fewer changes than another with which it may be compared, but it is not necessarily earlier in time. These distinctions are important for Saussure, because linguists before him did not pay attention to them, and, as a result, they erroneously put Sanskrit ahead of the Indo-European family of languages.

HIS BELIEFS CAN TRAP THE LINGUIST... UNLESS HE REMEMBERS THE OBJECT OF LINGUISTICS

Saussure also cautions that while the errors of earlier linguists have become apparent, there is some danger of perpetuating them. The comparative linguists were wrong to think of the evolution of language as a botanist thinks of the stages of growth of plant life. But this error is not eliminated if linguistics assumes that the "genius" of a race or ethnic group leads language through fixed stages of development. Saussure concluded his course with these observations, conceding that they are wholly negative. At the same time, they are of great use in emphasizing the whole point of his teaching:

THE TRUE AND UNIQUE OBJECT OF LINGUISTICS IS LANGUAGE STUDIED IN AND FOR ITSELF.

To What Extent Did *Saussure* Lay the Groundwork for Later Linguists?

ℰUROPEAN STRUCTURALISM

Saussure uses many comparisons in describing language: a symphony, a chess game, tapestry, wave-formation, etc. His favorite and most often repeated metaphor for the coherent body of knowledge that language-users draw on to speak or write is that of a **SYSTEM**. Sometimes he replaces this by **MECHANISM**. Curiously enough, the metaphor of **STRUCTURE** does not appear in Saussure's teachings, and yet the approach to linguistics for which he laid the groundwork came to be known as **STRUCTURALISM**. In linguistics, STRUCTURALISM is the study of language in its systematic aspects.

In Europe, STRUCTURALISM got its start in the 1920s, when **Roman Jakobson (1896-1982)** and other linguists declared their commitment to Saussure's view of language as system.

Jakobson and his associates gave their attention to the sounds of language, emphasizing the **relations** that exist between **distinctive** sounds--the ones that make a difference in **meaning**.

The key words in bold type here bring us back to Saussure's principles of SYNCHRONIC LINGUISTICS: CONTEXT and CONTRAST create SYNCHRONIC IDENTITY, the LINK between SOUND and THOUGHT produces FORM, the principle that distinguishes VALUE from MEANING distinguishes FORMS from each other and creates MEANING. All of these principles stem from Saussure's notion of the LINGUISTIC SIGN and remind us why he began his teaching with it.

Jakobson and his colleagues were confident enough in Saussure's basic idea of language as system to declare that the methods they were working out for describing sounds could be applied to other levels of linguistic analysis.

Gradually, these methods involved modifying almost all of Saussure's concepts to some extent.

The contrast between language system and speech was replaced by that of a code/message contrast. The synchronic/diachronic duality was eliminated in favor of a dynamic type of synchronic state that allows for linguistic change. Even the arbitrariness of the sign was challenged by exploring the idea of a motivated bond between the signifier and the signified, quite different from the limited type of motivation described by Saussure. In spite of these modifications, which seem to move structural linguistics away from Saussure, the duality of difference and opposition remains at the core of Jakobson's work and anchors it in the basic lessons of the CGL.

It is not difficult to find the echoes of Saussure

in Jakobson's writings, even many years after structuralism had been launched: *"Any sign is made up of constituent signs and/or occurs only in combination with other signs... . Any actual grouping of linguistic units binds them into a superior unit: combination and contexture are two faces of the same operation. A selection between alternatives implies the possibility of substituting one for the other, equivalent to the former in one respect and different from it in another. Actually, selection and substitution are two faces of the same operation."* (Fundamentals of Language, p. 60)

At the same time, Jakobson criticizes Saussure: *"The fundamental role which these two operations play in language was clearly realized by Ferdinand de Saussure. Yet from the two varieties of combination--concurrence and concatenation--it was only the latter, the temporal sequence, which was recognized by the Genevan linguist. Despite his own insight...the scholar succumbed to the traditional belief in the linear character of language."*

GUSTAVE GUILLAUME (1883-1960)

While Roman Jakobson worked closely with those who are identified as structural linguists, other European scholars followed separate paths. None more so than Gustave Guillaume. When Saussure's students published their master's teachings as the <u>CGL</u> in 1916, Guillaume was the first person to buy a copy in Paris. The book inspired him, as it did Jakobson, not to be an indoctrinated follower but to go beyond Saussure's seminal ideas.

Just as Jakobson replaced the language system/speech duality by the complementary concepts of code and message, Guillaume revised Saussure's principle. He spoke in his lectures of a shortcoming in that duality. His insight was that language-system is language in a potential state, and that speech is language as actualized. The link between potential and actual accounts for how language-users put words together to form sentences.

Guillaume's important innovation was in taking the static duality, language-system/speech, and turning it into a dynamic model of the human capacity for language. He did this by analyzing the operation between the language-system and speech that he called the **act** of language. This act involves time—the time required for a language-user to think the words of a message and say them. Distinguishing between language-system and language-activity, and

between these and the product of that activity,

Guillaume's operational model gave the framework for

a unique approach to linguistics. He developed this approach over a career spanning more than half a century and foreshadowing much contemporary work in cognitive analysis.

While the language-system/speech duality is superseded in Guillaume's work, other Saussurian principles remain intact. Just as in Saussure's account, Guillaume's describes the interaction of associations and linear relations.

Guillaume's operational model leads him to offer a criticism of the images of time related to Saussure's comparison between the synchronic/diachronic contrast and cutting across or down the stem of a plant:

"For Saussure, the two dominating images are those of time, which flows, and the instant, which immobilizes... This view is penetrating but rather summary. The systematizing that Saussure attributes to each immobilized instant in the progression of time is not in fact instantaneous: it took, takes and (since it changes) will take time, just as does the reverse process of disorganization, which prompts the systematization."

(*Foundations for a Science of Language*, p. 59)

So, while Guillaume keeps the associations/linear relations duality in his dynamic model of language, he reworks the synchronic/diachronic contrast, in order to show how the mind's systematic organizing operates on the

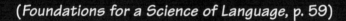

disorganization

created by linguistic change. At times, Guillaume's views seem to come close to undermining the most fundamental of Saussure's principles: *"I must diverge from Saussure's thought somewhat, [for] we are never really confronted with a system. The instant a system becomes established, it has virtually begun to remake itself."* (*Foundations for a Science of Language*, p. 60) Guillaume's solution to this problem is (again) to bring in the dimension of time: an operational analysis of synchronic states. For Guillaume, everything in language is operation, process, movement, or the result of these.

$\mathcal{P}$IERRE GUIRAUD (1912-1982)

After Guillaume, with structuralism flourishing in linguistics (and soon to be spilling over into other disciplines) in the 1950s, another French linguist put Saussure's principles to work in a new way. Like Jakobson and Guillaume, Guiraud brought the terms of Saussure's dualities together. He viewed the linguistic sign as arbitrary **and** motivated, form **and** substance. This was not so much a challenge to Saussure's views as an attempt to discover the full extent to which the vocabulary of a language is organized and interrelated.

Guiraud studied word-sets like the associative relations described by Saussure, but he confined himself to those where there is a similarity of **both** form and meaning: whirl, twirl, furl, curl, etc. Here all the words are linked by the general idea of a turning motion, and part of each word has the same sounds as all the others.

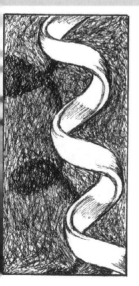

twirl

twist

curl

Going beyond standard language to dialect, and taking into account both current language and older words no longer in common use, Guiraud found an amazingly high percentage of the vocabulary to be structured. To the examples above (substituted for Guiraud's French examples), we may add stir, turn, twist, twine, purl, churn, quern, quirk, querl, coil, quoyle, etc. All these words express some variation on the idea of **turning**, as well as sharing sounds that form a continuum (the first and the last example do not have any sounds in common, but each word shares some sounds with some others).

Guiraud's view of the motivation of the linguistic sign is fundamentally different from Saussure's. The _CGL_ teaches that a sign is partially motivated when it is complex, when we can recognize its components and identify it as part of an associative series. For Guiraud, the sign does not have to be complex to be motivated; motivation can come from the associative series alone.

Even if a very large proportion of motivated words makes up the word-stock of a language, it does not under-mine Saussure's basic concept of the arbitrariness of the sign. If signs were not at least to some extent arbitrary, the form of language would be universal and changeless, which is not and never has been the case.

ℒ EONARD BLOOMFIELD (1887-1949)

Bloomfield, the linguist who founded American structuralism, wrote a favorable review of Saussure's _CGL_ in 1923. But Bloomfield's own book--_Language_ (1933)--refers to Saussure only once. The review shows why American structuralism would develop along completely different lines from European struc-turalism where Bloomfield states:

> I should differ from Saussure chiefly in basing my analysis on the sentence rather than on the word.

If linguistic analysis begins with the sentence, it does not require Saussure's emphasis on the signifier/signified duality and those related to it (meaning/ value, arbitrary/motivated). Bloomfield's

structuralism

is confined to the study of the visible structures of grammar and rejects abstract structures such as Saussure's notion of language-system, thus making the

language/speech

distinction irrelevant. On the subject of grammar, Saussure had nothing to say except that associative relations are the basis of grammatical categories. But the

language-system

is the key concept in his program for linguistics. Bloomfield wished to steer clear of such abstractions and also to avoid reference to mental entities in describing language. (This was the influence of behavioral psychology.)

As a consequence, he could not follow the lines of Saussure's sign-based approach. And whereas Saussure's method offered the prospect of discovering universal features of language, Bloomfield believed **all** languages would have to be fully described to provide evidence for such features. Does Bloomfield use **any** of the Saussurian dualities? No, not in his synchronic analysis of language, but unlike a later generation of American linguists, he did not exclude diachronic linguistics.

*N*OAM CHOMSKY (1928-)

When Chomsky broke on the linguistic scene with a little book called

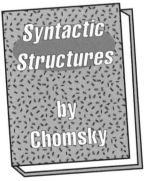

in 1957, American structuralism was in its heyday, and Saussure was already being discovered by researchers in areas outside linguistics. Chomsky, trained in the tradition of Bloomfield and his followers, was oriented to a grammar-based approach to linguistics. In *Syntactic Structures* he began to work out a new type of analysis called **transformational generative grammar**. The name means a model of grammar that **generates**, or produces, all the possible sentences of a language and shows how a sentence can be **transformed** into another one by applying certain rules.

93

Having been trained in America, Chomsky learned practically nothing of Saussure, discovering him only after the first English translation of the _CGL_ appeared in 1959. Chomsky's career can be divided into three phases from that time onward. The status of Saussure in Chomsky's thinking varies with the progression through the three phases.

In his earliest r e f e r - e n c e   t o   Saussure, Chomsky focuses on the language/speech duality, stressing what he views as a shortcoming:

Saussure's conclusion that sentence structure belongs to speech rather than to the language-system prevents him from developing systematic rules for sentence function. Chomsky's own conception of the language-system is that of a generative process. The metaphor of a g e n e r a t i n g device is used only marginally in Saussure, and not in Chomsky's technical sense of a set of ordered rules that are applied repeatedly in a fixed order to produce sentences.

The contrast between Saussure's general interest in how language functions and Chomsky's specific interest in syntax accounts for Chomsky's dissatisfaction with Saussure's approach to describing the language-system. But in spite of his criticisms, Chomsky invokes Saussure as an authority to support the program of generative grammar.

Beginning in 1973, and for over a decade, I stopped referring to Saussure altogether.

By 1986, scattered references to Saussure's concept of the language-system begin to reappear in his writings. It is characterized as appropriate but too narrow, because it does not account for linguistic creativity (the fact that we learn to create an infinite variety of sentences from a limited number of models).

Chomsky also seems, in this third phase of his career, to have finally dropped the criticism, so often repeated in the first phase, that Saussure viewed language as a system of elements rather than as a system of rules.

How did Saussure's ideas make their way beyond linguistics?

6 LAUDE LÉVI STRAUSS (1906 -)

American structuralism began to decline as the dominant methodology in linguistics, as a result of Chomsky's innovations, but it had already migrated to other disciplines, especially in Europe. Lévi-Strauss, an anthropologist, had learned of Saussure's work through Roman Jakobson and had contributed an article, "Structural Analysis in Linguistics and Anthropology," to the journal *Word*, launched by Jakobson in 1945.

Word

Roman Jakobson, Ed.

Structuralism as the dominant methodology in linguistics.

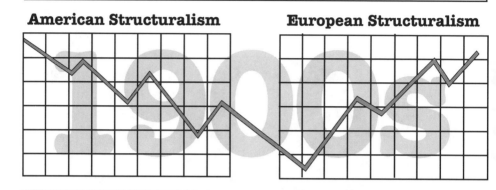

Lévi-Strauss took an immediate interest in Jakobson's teachings about the sound-system of language, because he considered distinctive sound units as the point of intersection between nature and culture.

By the 1960s, his application of Saussurian principles to social anthropology was so firmly entrenched and widely known that he began to rival Saussure for the title of **"father of structuralism."** Anthropology lent itself to those principles because of the constant interplay of similarities and differences which

Father of the Year

emerge from the comparison of different societies.

And society itself is comparable to a synchronic system. It may be described in the way that Saussure envisaged the description of a state of language--as the interaction of its various features.

A synchronic view takes precedence in anthropology as in linguistics, and for the same reason. The history of a people is irrelevant to the daily operation of their social structure, just as the history of a language-system is irrelevant to its functioning **as a system**. Lévi-Strauss goes beyond the data of anthropology, just as Saussure seeks to understand the universal principles behind the variety of individual languages.

Lévi-Strauss approaches the study of kinship, a traditional concern of anthropologists, from a viewpoint which owes much to the Saussurian duality of meaning/value.

"Like phonemes [distinctive sounds], kinship terms are elements of meaning; like phonemes, they acquire meaning only if they are integrated into systems. 'Kinship systems', like 'phonetic systems', are built by the mind on the level of unconscious thought. Finally, the recurrence of kinship patterns, marriage rules, similar prescribed attitudes between certain types of relatives, and so forth, in scattered regions of the globe and in fundamentally different societies, leads us to believe that, in the case of kinship as well as linguistics, the observable phenomena result from the action of laws which are general but implicit."

(*Structural Anthropology*, p. 34)

Other Saussurian principles also figure prominently in Lévi-Strauss. When he studies myth, his analysis is structural and consists of the elements of myth viewed synchronically as a set of logical relations; from the diachronic point of view, structure is the relationships of transposition, inversion, etc., among contrasting myths.

Lévi-Strauss also makes use of the concept of motivation, noting that whereas for Saussure language moves from arbitrariness to motivation, in myth the movement is from motivation to arbitrariness, because new, external elements are added.

Finally, Saussure's principle that signs are not abstract but real entities is transposed by Lévi-Strauss to the claim that structures are real entities in the brain.

ℛOLAND BARTHES (1915-1980)

Barthes and Lévi-Strauss have been called the true structuralists.

Trained in French literature and classics, Barthes wrote, during the early stage of his career, on themes in sociology, lexicology (vocabulary studies), and literary criticism. He discovered Saussure in 1957 and was stimulated to write over seventy articles by 1963, repeatedly applying the Saussurian concepts of sign, signified, and signifier. In 1964 came *Elements of Semiology*, a full-blown account of all the key notions in Saussure and the rich variety of applications that Barthes saw for them. These new avenues were opened up by a radical first step:

"We must now face the possibility of inverting Saussure's declaration: Linguistics is not part of the general science of signs, even a privileged part, it is semiology which is a part of linguistics; to be precise, it is that part covering the **great signifying unities** of discourse. By this inversion we may expect to bring to light the unity of the research at present being done in anthropology, sociology, psycho-analysis and stylistics round the concept of signification."

(*Elements of Semiology*, p. 11)

The discussion of Saussure's principles as **linguistic** principles is probably richer in Barthes than in any other writer who appropriated them for use outside linguistics. Barthes quickly switches from exposition to application, using the Saussurian notion of system, for example, to describe clothing, cars, furniture, etc. "Let us now take another signifying system: **food**. We shall find there without difficulty Saussure's distinction."

"The alimentary language is made of: **i)** rules of exclusion (alimentary taboos): **ii)** signifying oppositions of units, the type of which remains to be determined (for instance the type **savory/sweet**); **iii)** rules of association, either simultaneous (at the level of a dish) or successive (at the level of a menu); **iv)** rituals of use which function, perhaps, as a kind of alimentary **rhetoric**." (*Elements of Semiology*, pp. 27-8)

It becomes clear why Barthes, in this phase of his writing, has shared with Lévi-Strauss the label of "true structuralist." In later phases of his work, he moves on to other interests without repudiating either Saussure's teachings or the use he has made of them himself.

JACQUES LACAN (1901-1981)

Lacan, a surrealist poet, recycled himself as a psycho-analyst. Influenced by Jakobson, he brought out points of connection between Freudianism and structuralism and affirmed the linguistic basis of psychoanalysis. He developed the notion of **symbolic order** for the interaction of patient and analyst

from the fundamental notion of communication through signs. This is a general concept that could have developed with no help from Saussure, but Lacan turns to the <u>CGL</u> as a starting point for a much more specific idea.

Whereas Barthes reversed Saussure's view of the relationship between linguistics and semiotics, Lacan turns Saussure's diagram for the linguistic sign upside down.

SOMETIMES A SIGN IS JUST A SIGN.

signified / **signifier**   **becomes**   **S** / **s**

The upper **S** is the signifier, and the lower (and deliberately smaller) s is the signified. The purpose of this change is to ensure that the signifier is not viewed as if its primary function is simply and automatically to represent the signified. The line separating the two parts of the sign in Saussure's diagram is not only retained by Lacan but becomes functional and symbolic of the blocked connection between signifier and signified when language is disturbed by neurosis, dementia, etc.

Lacan's revision of Saussure's diagram suits the purposes of psychoanalysis, but as a revision of the linguistic principle put forward by Saussure it is neither necessary nor relevant. It simply overlooks Saussure's basic teaching that the function of language is not to create a sound medium for the expression of thought but to mediate between thought and sound--a lesson that Lacan would have done well to absorb before "c o r r e c t i n g" S a u s s u r e. Nevertheless, at least one linguist, Françoise Gadet, believes that Lacan has improved on the _CGL_ by providing a full and genuinely Saussurian interpretation of the notion of linguistic value.

Lacan used Saussure's concepts of **associative** and **linear relations** among words to demonstrate that aphasia resulting in disrupted associations blocks a patient's ability to find words to complete a grammatical structure, whereas aphasia related to linear structures blocks the grammatical structure itself.

Derrida, a French philosopher, is generally acknowledged as the founder of **post-structuralism** (also called **deconstruction**)-- an attempt to correct some of the perceived shortcomings of structuralism. Derrida's arguments pinpoint three areas of Saussure's thought requiring correction:

- his idealism,
- his emphasis on spoken language, and
- his use of binary oppositions (we have been calling them **dualities**) to describe language.

By **idealism** Derrida means the view that language does not create meanings but simply reveals them. He imputes this view to Saussure in disregard of the same key point in the _CGL_ that Lacan missed-- the language-system as a mediator between sound and thought. Both thought and sound are formless, Saussure taught, until they are linked and acquire form through the creation of those links-- called signs. There are no pre-existing meanings in this view, as Derrida believes.

Derrida attaches primary importance to the concept of

DIFFERENCE

which is also fundamental for Saussure, but he does not retain the complementary term **opposition**.

He also follows Saussure in making **system** a basic notion. On the basis of **system** and **difference**, D e r r i d a develops the concept of **archi-writing**--a system of pure differentiality that underlies writing **and** speaking. He charges that Saussure did not recognize such a system, because of his prejudiced view of writing as nothing more than a derived way of representing speech. To call Saussure's view of writing a prejudice is to disregard his whole purpose of avoiding the endless confusion and errors in the work of earlier linguists, who had always limited themselves to written texts.

Derrida rejects Saussure's procedure of working with complementary pairs of terms such as associative and linear relations. This pair, especially, is related to the even more fundamental duality of absence/presence that Derrida banishes as a starting point for deconstruction.

The whole project of eliminating dualities becomes unnecessary when we recall that Saussure concluded his lesson on linear relations and associations by showing how they interact. They are defined independently, but they operate interdependently. Since definitions are particularly subject to the endless play of signifiers (a normal state of affairs, according to the post-structuralist view), there is no point to objecting to their provisionally independent status in Saussurian linguistics. Saussure moved beyond all his dualities himself. In this sense, he deconstructed structuralism more than half a century before Derrida.

What was *Saussure* doing when he wasn't doing linguistics?

At the time that he began lecturing on general linguistics in 1907, Saussure was already compulsively filling notebook after notebook with his exercises in decoding Horace, Virgil, and other Latin authors.

Why did they need decoding? Because Saussure believed their writings were based on key words (often people's names) or phrases, split up and hidden in the visible words. He called these **anagrams**.

The Scene: *Saussure is in his bathrobe, poring over a pile of notebooks in his study. Clock shows 2 a.m. Madame Saussure calls from upstairs...*

Ferdinand! Still anguishing over anagrams, my prince? Lots of hugs if you come to bed now!

Saussure transcribes her words and thinks to himself...

Is there a name hidden here? Is it really me she's calling to bed?

He sits in silence for a long time and then boxes the letters as shown.

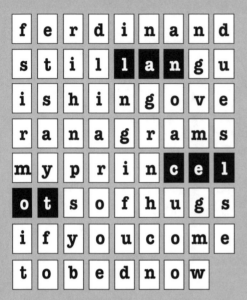

f	e	r	d	i	n	a	n	d
s	t	i	l	**l**	**a**	**n**	g	u
i	s	h	i	n	g	o	v	e
r	a	n	a	g	r	a	m	s
m	y	p	r	i	n	**c**	**e**	l
o	**t**	s	o	f	h	u	g	s
i	f	y	o	u	c	o	m	e
t	o	b	e	d	n	o	w	

Aha! Lancelot is her lover!

The clock now shows 3:10 a.m. Madame S calls again...

FERDINAND! I CALLED YOU OVER AN HOUR *AGO*. FOR HEAVEN'S SAKE COME TO BED NOW!

...scramble...
...scrambe...
...scramble...

Oh, my *God!* She's seeing *Iago* too!

...then up the stairs he went... .

Saussure suggested a lot of complicated rules for how the anagrams operate. The key word or phrase was supposed to split up as many different ways as possible and each of these fragments was then supposed to be repeated as many times as possible. If Madame Saussure really was using *Lancelot* as her key word, she would then use other words containing **la-, lan-, -ance**, etc.

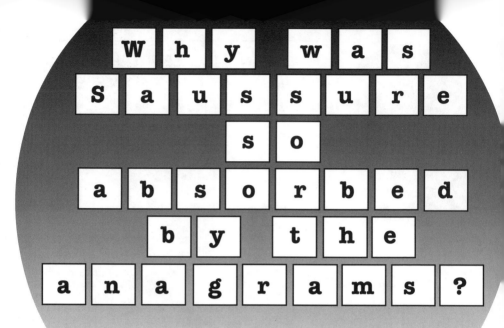

Why was Saussure so absorbed by the anagrams?

We can only speculate. Some scholars believe that his frustration over the incomplete and untidy state of his research on the subject (over a hundred notebooks containing mainly fragments) made him turn to linguistics, in the belief that it lent itself more readily to the discovery of system. Others believe that (deliberately or not) he undermined some of his linguistic concepts such as the arbitrariness of the sign and the linearity of the signifier with the notion of the anagram.

What is clear at least is that linguistics and the anagrams come together in the big question with which Saussure was concerned: The language system exists to serve speech, to supply its elements, but what separates speech from the language system? **Here we are very nearly back to asking whether the chicken or the egg came first.** In the _CGL_ Saussure shows us his intuitions for answering this type of question; with the anagrams he complicates the question slightly by asking us to think about omelets.

108

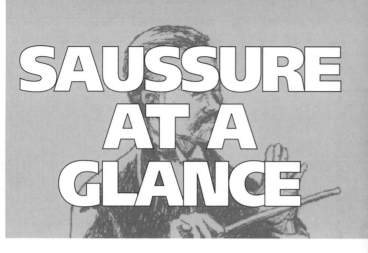

SAUSSURE AT A GLANCE

1. The definition of language (the language system)

The _CGL_ does not reduce its view of language to one tidy statement or repeat any key phrase to describe it. Instead, one finds lessons touching on various aspects of language that include a sentence beginning **"Language is... ."** They may be summarized as follows:

Language is

... simultaneously a social product of the human capacity for speech and a set of necessary conventions.

... a unified and self-contained whole and a principle of classification.

... something acquired and conventional.

... distinct from speaking and can be studied independently.

... a system of sounds where the only essential element is the link between meaning and sound-image.

... a system governed by its own internal order.

... the human capacity for speech minus speaking.

... a system of pure values determined by nothing other than a given state of its own elements.

... a mechanism which continues to operate even when it deteriorates.

... a system whose parts can and must all be considered in their synchronic unity.

... a system of interrelated elements, where the value of one derives only from the simultaneous presence of the others.

Saussure also said what language is **not**:

LANGUAGE IS NOT A MECHANISM CREATED WITH A VIEW TO THE IDEAS TO BE EXPRESSED.

Why didn't I read Saussure more carefully? Why didn't they have **For Beginners** when I was beginning?

Derrida

2. Comparisons Saussure makes to help us understand language and linguistics

We looked at several of these earlier:

planets in the solar system

chess

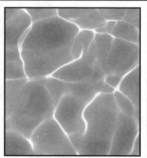

the chemistry of water

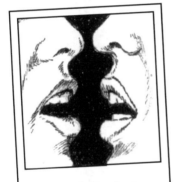

exchanges

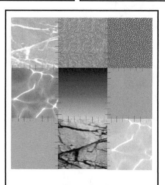

patched cloth

Here are some more:

A Symphony

Language is like a symphony. The reality of language as a system of expression is separate from the use people make of it, just as the reality of a symphony is independent of its performance by musicians.

A Dictionary

Language is like a dictionary whose contents are stored in the minds of speakers. (It is important to remember that not just words are stored in speakers' minds but everything they need to know-- rules for word formation, grammar, etc.-- to be able to communicate.)

Plant Life

Just as the internal structure of a plant is altered by external factors such as soil and climate, grammatical structure depends on external factors of linguistic change.

Faces and Photographs

Language users attach so much more importance to the written word than to the spoken word that it is as if one believed that you could know a person better from looking at her photograph than at her face.

A Life Belt

This attachment to written language is so strong that taking it away is like depriving a beginning swimmer of his life belt.

A Tapestry

The oppositions between sound-images in the language system are like the visual oppositions between threads of different color in a tapestry.

3. How Saussure describes the concept of linguistic value

Like the concept of the language system, that of linguistic value is characterized by Saussure in several different ways:

Linguistic value is the position of an element of language relative to others.

Linguistic value is the elements of language keeping each other in equilibrium.

The value of a linguistic sign derives solely from the simultaneous presence of other signs.

The value of a linguistic sign is really determined by what exists outside it.

Linguistic value is defined as words for related ideas limiting each other's meanings by the contrasts among them.

The linguistic value of any given word is determined by those related to it.

4. Writing and Linguistic Signs

Saussure presents an important contrast between two types of writing systems. The difference between them is best understood in terms of the linguistic sign.

Ideographic Writing

In this system, of which Chinese is an example, the linguistic sign is represented by a unique symbol which is completely different from all the other symbols of the writing system. It is not related to the sounds of the sign. (If you know Chinese and you see the character for "cat," you get the idea, but the shape of the character does not tell you how to pronounce it.) It is directly linked to the idea it stands for.

Phonetic Writing

In this system, of which English is an example, the linguistic sign is represented by a symbol (sequence of letters) which is **not** completely different from other symbols, because the same letters are used in different combinations for other words. It **is** related to the sounds of the sign. It is a link to the sounds of the sign and through them **indirectly** linked to the idea it stands for.

5. Saussure's dualities
(in order of presentation)

These contrasting pairs of terms that Saussure used to organize his approach to linguistics are probably the best known feature of his work.

They are listed here to give an overview and for quick reference. The numbers in brackets refer to the pages of this book where the dualities are discussed.

1) language/speech (**langue/parole** in the original French) .... (p. 16)

2) signifier/signified .... (p. 22)

3) synchronic/diachronic .... (p. 30)

4) form/substance .... (p. 46)

5) meaning/value .... (p. 46)

6) difference/opposition .... (p. 52)

7) linear relations/associative relations .... (p. 53)

8) arbitrary/motivated .... (p. 25/56)

Question:

Can you recognize any of the principles that Saussure taught in the following report?

"WORDS CALLED 'KEY TO ASIAN MATH SKILLS'"

East Asian preschoolers are better at mathematics than children who speak European languages because their words for numbers are not intrinsically confusing, newly published research indicates.

A study of 197 three- to five-year olds in China and in the U.S. showed that the two groups learned to count to 10 equally well, but that a huge chasm opened when they counted higher.

The research, by psychologists at the University of Illinois at Urbana and at Beijing Normal University, points out that between the numbers 1 and 10 the words in Chinese and English are equally arbitrary.

"One cannot predict that *nine* follows *eight* or that *jiu* follows *ba*," the authors say.

However, after 10, English becomes irregular in two ways. The words eleven and twelve have only a historical relationship to one and two. More troubling for children is that then they are faced with a teen system--a word category that is never used again. In Chinese, however, the number for 11 translates as "ten one," for twelve as "ten two," and so on.

One experiment demonstrated how the teen numbers work havoc in abstract counting. The children were asked to count as high as they could in serial order starting with one, two, three. Although 94 percent of the American children and 92 percent of the Chinese could count to 10 without making a mistake, only 48 percent of the former reached 20, whereas 74 percent of the latter did.

The reason the U.S. children were confused, Illinois psychologist Kevin Miller says, is that "in the teens in English, there is no sign that you have passed a numerical boundary [at the number 10] and that you are using a 10-based system."

Further evidence of that problem was a test that showed the two groups of children were equally matched when counting piles of stones representing numbers between three and ten. However, at the age of five, 40 percent of English speakers made mistakes when the piles went up to 17. Not one of the Chinese five-year olds had this sort of problem.

In soon-to-be presented research, the group will report that the gap found between English and Chinese also exists between Chinese and European languages.

In French, there is an irregular 11, 12, 13, 14, 15, 16 and a teen system for 17, 18, 19. But beyond that, 70 becomes soixante-dix (sixty-ten), 80 becomes quatre-vingt (four-twenty), and 91 is spoken as quatre-vingt-onze (four-twenty-eleven).

Emphasizing that language differences don't explain all observed differences between East Asian and European abilities in mathematics, Professor Miller said there were two clear policy implications to his work.

"Obviously we would make life easier for our children if 14 could become something like onedy four," he said. "But that is not going to happen."

-- The Globe & Mail
16 March 1995

Answer:

1. There are more arbitrary signs among the names for the numbers in English than there are in Chinese.

2. Changes in pronunciation in English for 1 and 11, 2 and 12, have been so great that we don't recognize their connections. The motivated signs for 11 and 12 turned into arbitrary signs.

3. There are more arbitrary signs among the names for the teen numbers in French than there are in English.

4. In the final quotation, the professor understands that the sign is unchangeable by design. Saussure explains that this unchangeable quality of the sign is due to its arbitrariness.

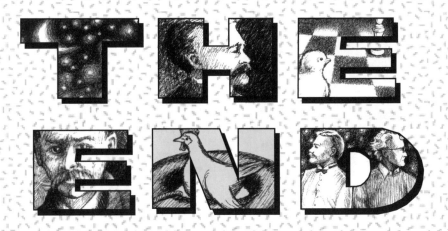

QUOTED WORKS

BARTHES, Roland. *Elements of Semiology.* London: Cape, 1967.

BLOOMFIELD, Leonard. "Review of Ferdinand de Saussure. *Cours de linguistique générale.*" *Modern Language Journal,* 8 (1923), pp. 317-19.

GUILLAUME, Gustave. *Foundations for a Science of Language.* Amsterdam/Philadelphia: John Benjamins, 1984.

JAKOBSON, Roman, and Morris Halle. *Fundamentals of Language.* The Hague: Mouton, 1956.

LÉVI-STRAUSS, Claude. *Structural Anthropology.* New York: Basic Books, 1963.

SUGGESTED READINGS FOR BEGINNERS

HARRIS, Roy. *Reading Saussure.* London: Duckworth, 1987.

STURROCK, John. *Structuralism.* London: Collins, 1986.

STURROCK, John, ed. *Structuralism and Since.* Oxford: Oxford University Press, 1979.

READINGS FOR THE CONVERTED AND THE INTREPID

ANGENOT, Marc. "Structuralism as Syncretism: Institutional Distortions of Saussure." In John Fekete, ed., *The Structural Allegory* (Minneapolis: University of Minnesota Press, 1984), pp. 150-163.

BERMAN, Art. *From the New Criticism to Deconstruction.* Chicago: University of Illinois Press, 1988.

BOON, James A. *From Symbolism to Structuralism.* New York: Harper and Row, 1972.

CULLER, Jonathan. *Ferdinand de Saussure.* Ithaca, N.Y.: Cornell University Press, 1986.

DEELY, John. *Basics of Semiotics.* Bloomington: Indiana University Press, 1990.

GADET, Françoise. *Saussure and Contemporary Culture.* London: Hutchinson, 1989.

KOERNER, E. F. Konrad. "Chomsky's readings of the *Cours de linguistique générale.*" *Lingua e Stile* 29, 2 (1994), pp. 267-84.

KOERNER, E.F. Konrad. *Ferdinand de Saussure: Origin and Development of His Linguistic Thought in Western Studies of Language.* Braunschweig: F. Vieweg, 1973.

STAROBINSKI, Jean. *Words upon Words: The Anagrams of Ferdinand de Saussure.* New Haven, Conn.: Yale University Press, 1979.

STEINER, George. *Real Presences.* Chicago: University of Chicago Press, 1989.

STROZIER, Robert. *Saussure, Derrida and the Metaphysics of Subjectivity.* Berlin: Mouton de Gruyter, 1988.

meaning, 42–43, 46, 49, 58, 69, 74
exchange of, 48
Meillet, Antoine, 5
message, 85
motivated sign, 56–58, 68, 73, 75

name, 21
nomenclature theory, 18–21
non-linear relation, 53
numbers, words used for, 117–19

Ogden, C. K., 23–24, 37

paired terms See dualities parole, 16–17
pattern, 54–58, 70
philology, 12
phonetic changes, 59–72
  mediated, 61
  theories about causes of, 61–64
phonetic writing, 115–16
phonology, 18
Pictet, Adolphe, 3
Plato, 12
psychoanalysis, 101–2

racial theories of language change, 61
Richards, I. A., 23–24, 37, 38

Saussure, Ferdinand de
  academic career, 3–5
  family background, 2–3
  influence of, in linguistics and other fields, 4–6, 11, 16–17, 50, 82–104
  interest in anagrams, 105–8
  linguistic studies and methods, 15–17
  works and writings, 1–6
sentence, 91–92, 94
sequence of sounds, 38
series of forms, 75
Shakespeare, William, 12

sign, 13–14, 17, 38–40, 52, 72, 101
  two-part, 38–40 See also linguistic sign
signified, 22–30, 38–40, 46, 52, 101–2
signifier, 22–30, 38–40, 46, 52, 101–2
sign-sequence, 53
simple sign, 56–58
sound, 44, 48, 51
  difference in, and meaning, 49
speech, 17, 19–20, 38–40, 51, 73, 86, 94
  linearity of, 53
structuralism, 83–86, 91–104
synchronic fact, 69
synchronic linguistics, 30–58
system. See language, as system

thing, 21
thought, 44, 117–19
transformational generative grammar, 37, 93–95

value, 41–43, 46–48
vowels, 3–4, 61

Webster, Noah, 12
Whewell, William, 12
Whitney, Dwight, 12
Wilkins, John, 12
words association among, 54–58
  changing meanings of, 29–30
  distinct sounds of, 49
  etymology of, 66–68, 76–79
  linguistic units contained in, 40–41
  phonetic analogies among, 89–91
  See also linguistic signwriting, 104
  ideographic vs. phonetic, 115–16